BEFORE I LEAVE

BEFORE I LEAVE

JENNEY EGERTSON

Wise Ink Creative Publishing

ISBN 13: 978-1-63489-167-7
LCCN: 2018956994
Printed in the United States of America
First Printing: 2018

22 21 20 19 18 5 4 3 2 1

Cover design by Alison Forner
Interior design by Patrick Maloney

Wise Ink Creative Publishing replaces every tree used in printing their books by planting thousands of trees every year in reforestation programs. Learn more at wiseink.com.

When women of all ages come together and talk—really talk, openly and without ego—a certain magic happens. Older women realize their vast collection of mundane moments add up to great wisdom. Younger women see that they're not doing anything wrong; life simply is sad and joyful and complicated. And we women in the very hard middle part learn to relax a little, quit punishing ourselves and see beauty in aging. These gatherings are filled with hope. That's what Jenney Egertson's *Before I Leave* is like. It's filled with the steadfast love of women who survived heartbreaking childhoods and long marriages, answering the questions we're all asking. And threaded through is a brave narrative voice, a woman navigating midlife and measuring her own choices against the stories she hears. This is a book for every woman who wants to sit around a table and feel the sisterhood of women who've been there. "It's hard sometimes," they admit when Egertson asks. "But don't worry, you're doing fine."

—Ann Bauer, author of *The Forever Marriage*

TABLE OF CONTENTS

story - **stawr**-ee or **stohr**-ee, noun
A narrative, either true or fictitious, in prose or verse, designed to interest, amuse, or instruct the hearer or reader; a tale.

STORIES THAT HEAL

Maude Kelly

BY 2:00 A.M., the houses surrounding a small city park near downtown Philadelphia had been dark for hours. A young constable rode slowly through the silent square on horseback. Anticipating how good it would feel to hand over his late-night shift to the next guy, he almost missed the tiny figure moving unsteadily among the trees. But a breaking branch and the soft sounds of what he thought must be a small animal caught his attention. He swung his horse toward the sound and dismounted, expecting to find a stray cat. But when he directed his light toward the sound, the young man blinked hard as he bent down to face the knee-high intruder. Standing before him was a small child—a girl, age three. It was 2:05 a.m. and she was alone.

Seventy-seven years later, Maude Kelly and I would be introduced at a party held in her honor.

IT WAS EARLY June of 2000 when I drove from Minneapolis to Chicago to retrieve my teenage daughter, Rowan, who had spent a few days with our friends Kate and Fran. The night before we started back, Kate hosted a birthday celebration for the eighty-year-old mother of a close friend and colleague. We were just finishing dinner when I asked whether anyone among our small group of six women thought that "feminism" had become a dirty word during the last couple of decades.

There we were—three generations of women—about to share what it felt like to live as a female under "patriarchy"—another word I normally saved for a few feminist friends. The two professors were articulate but careful. Fran applied dry humor to stories of her life as an out lesbian in 1960s St. Louis. Rowan left the table after a few minutes.

But there was one voice I didn't recognize from my earlier years as a feminist—one story I hadn't heard a million times: eighty-year-old Maude Kelly's. Not that she opposed anything being said—she strongly agreed with all of us. It was her point of view as a survivor that got my attention, and her calm, matter-of-fact resolve. Here was a woman, born shortly after World War I, who had watched her gender navigate the years before, during, and after the women's movement. While I didn't recognize the voice, I was drawn to its wisdom. Which is why, when Maude and her daughter Beth prepared to leave shortly after dinner, I felt strangely and acutely sad. As we said goodbye, I made a mental note to tell Kate that somehow, somewhere, I had to see Maude again. I had the sense that our conversation wasn't finished.

That sense continued the next day on the road as I thought of ways to approach Maude—maybe I would write an essay about her. Perhaps I could interview not only Maude but other women as well, women who were close to her age. "What if I wrote a book of chapters containing the stories and advice of a small but diverse group of women?" I asked myself. "What if I gave that generation of women a voice?" And then, in a flash of clairvoyance that happens to me about once every five years, the words "Before I Leave" appeared like a vision. That's when I knew I would write about women. What I didn't understand yet was why.

The following January I finally had the nerve to call Maude, who sounded genuinely happy to hear from me. Would she be willing to let me interview her? Could I tell her story and pass on her advice? Claiming she had little of interest to say, she agreed nevertheless.

In June of 2001, I booked a flight to Philadelphia.

"WHAT A CUTE place," I said, stepping into Maude's entryway more than a year after our first meeting. As I stood beside her and looked around the apartment, I noticed the contrast between Maude's decorating style and her choice in clothing. The crisp, tailored shirt Maude wore neatly tucked into perfectly-fitting slacks seemed almost masculine compared to the soft, more feminine pinks and mauves she had chosen for her living room.

"Well, I won't complain," replied Maude modestly. "You wouldn't believe what I'd pay anywhere else."

I was beginning to notice details now—a comfortable couch, photos of grandkids, several framed pieces of needlework, and one small window throwing light across a longish rectangular space that served as both living and dining room. For two people, it would be tight. For Maude, it was perfect. She and I seemed to have a few things in common, too, like the way we used color and fabric to decorate—a good omen, I thought, as I prepared to barrage Maude with questions over the next two days.

"Who does the needlepoint?" I asked.

"Oh, some is mine and some is Beth's," said Maude. I could tell she was proud of her daughter, of the needlepoint, of her apartment. "Welcome to my home," she said, opening her arms.

Two hours later we were seated at Maude's favorite restaurant—a cheerful, unpretentious establishment called Sam's Clam

Bar, located on Somer's Point and famous locally for its seafood entrees. I admired Maude's confidence and sense of place as she greeted our server, and even a few patrons. I envied the obvious pride Maude showed for her hometown and was eager to hear about her experiences as a longtime inhabitant. It all fit with what I remembered about Maude's modern sensibilities, and her independence as a single woman.

By the time we dropped off Maude's car at her apartment on the way to the beach, I could tell she was comfortable. I felt relieved that I wouldn't have to drag information out of her, but also appreciated the boundaries she set around discussing her children—we wouldn't do a lot of that. Best of all, this well-kept woman was starting to feel like a friend.

Finally we reached the Boardwalk. And that's when I began to see Ocean City through Maude's eyes. Walking past an endless line of souvenir and tattoo booths, she fondly remembered the collection of 1940s clothing, jewelry, and knitting boutiques that used to be there—I loved her artistic descriptions of the trends and styles that were popular in her day. She brought to life the miles of fishing cabins that once lined the beach, tiny, hopeful structures where hundreds of families would experience feast or famine during the coming year based on a single short season.

"You mean they didn't have work during the rest of the year?" I asked, imagining how anxious a mother with six children might feel.

"Many of them didn't," answered Maude. "It was really tough for some of them."

When Maude turned to her childhood, I imagined her skipping across the sand as a seven-year-old. Her voice flattened when she told me her mother had "finally" brought her daughter to the beach only after learning that Maude had a severe case of rickets.

"Isn't that something kids get when they're not receiving the nutrients they need?"

"Yes, it is," she replied somewhat sharply, expressing a surprising level of disapproval.

I thought the moment had passed when Maude mentioned how much she had later enjoyed watching her own children play on the beach. I knew I was wrong when her voice took on a sarcastic, singsong quality as she explained what it meant to be the only daughter of Jules and Ethel Hatman. And when she lowered her voice to describe the regular beatings she received as a child, I felt the force of her mother's fist.

By that time we were almost back to her apartment, but I couldn't let Maude stop her story there, so I asked if we could continue for a few more minutes.

"Tomorrow, honey," she said, sounding tired. "We'll talk more tomorrow."

THE NEXT MORNING, we sat down after breakfast. Born on May 22, 1920, Maude spent the first several years of her life without a name. And while she spoke with great affection of her father, even Jules called his daughter "girlie" until the day he was required to come up with an official name for his child.

Meanwhile, Maude believed from an early age that her mother, Ethel, preferred her two sons. One brother was five years older—by the time his sister was born he had already been through thirteen operations to correct a cleft palate and harelip. "As far as I was concerned, he was very good-looking," recalled Maude. "But after I grew up I realized he was also a pain in the neck!"

I knew all about "pain in the neck" brothers. I let her continue.

"They weren't very nice to me," said Maude, who went on to describe the two beautiful dolls she had received from relatives—one from Germany and one from England. "My brother was allowed to cut their hair and push their eyes in and break them."

Reliving my own sibling battles, I asked, somewhat heatedly, why he was allowed to do that. When she described her brother as a "mama's boy" who was waited on hand and foot by his older sister, I wondered aloud whether he was favored because of all the operations.

Maude nodded in confirmation that Ethel had probably felt she had to protect her vulnerable son. As a mother myself, I could understand that instinct. In my role as sister, I was annoyed. Especially because, according to Maude, her younger brother was a mama's boy too, while Maude remained mostly on her own.

"I wandered around the neighborhood park even after dark," she said. "That went on until the night the mounted police picked me up in Fairmount Park."

That was the moment I knew for sure that Maude's story would not be a happy one. I felt outrage: What kind of parents allow a three-year-old to wander outside alone after dark, or even during the day? Why wouldn't at least one of them have made sure Maude was safely in bed? How could they not know—or care—where she was?

Maude never found out how the bewildered officer discovered where she lived, but those were most certainly the questions he had asked as he handed over the sleepy little girl to her parents. The child was dirty. She was hungry. She hadn't known where she was as she climbed into the arms of a man she didn't even recognize. What he did know was that Jules and Ethel would be required to have their daughter supervised at all times from that moment on. He would make sure of it.

Not that the house was empty. "There were always lots of people staying over," said Maude as she finished her story. "Every weekend was party time."

I caught the reference to alcohol and knew it might explain the neglect. But Maude claimed she never felt neglected; in fact, several times during my stay Maude would mention her father's care and kindness, how he bathed her until she was four, and how much she loved him.

Imagining a loving father bent over an old-fashioned tub, I asked where Ethel would have been during those times, to which Maude replied that as a young child she hardly saw her mother. "She was not the type of mother who brushed your hair and helped you put your clothes on," said Maude. "Usually she was late in getting up because she was hungover."

That triggered a split second of intense anger for me. While Maude had left her childhood rage behind, I apparently had not done the same with mine. On that particular day I was easily able to bury feelings of dread about my recent decision to enter round two of an alcoholic marriage; but Maude's story had resurrected a memory and feelings I thought I had resolved long ago. Now, in front of Maude, both emotions and ancient images associated with an incident that occurred when I was four years old had returned.

In 1958, my family lived in southern California on a sunny street with fragrant, eye-level flowers and brilliant green lawns that spelled paradise to a barefoot four-year-old. To keep me occupied while my mother prepared for another new baby, my parents had given me a full-size doll with dark brown hair—I loved that doll. But one day I stood on the side of our house where I believed I wouldn't be seen, took off all my doll's clothes, and struck her pliable body against the ground as hard as I could. Over and over I lifted the doll above my head before smashing her cruelly against the lawn, the sidewalk, and the side of the house. I knew I shouldn't be doing it—how could I punish my beautiful doll in that way? Worse yet, I only became angrier and guiltier with each ruthless blow.

For decades that memory was always accompanied by shame; eventually, I recognized that around that time I had lost something important . . . and that I had directed my anger toward the doll, who couldn't strike back or punish me. Of course, I wouldn't have talked about it—little girls didn't do such things. Good girls weren't cruel to others, either. I believed it was wrong to be that angry. Much as I wanted to, I knew I must never do that again. Instead, I would swallow my anger. I would silence my voice.

Maude brought me back to our conversation when she mentioned the year her youngest brother was born. After that, eight-year-old Maude got no attention from Ethel and stayed out of her way. "Most of the time I annoyed my mother, and then it was a beating . . . she was quick with her hands," explained Maude.

"You mean she would hit you with her hand," I repeated.

"Oh, or anything she had in her hands."

Maude's story was also stirring up for me some very old feelings about the various ways boys were favored over girls. So I asked whether Ethel also struck her sons. When Maude said the beatings were reserved for her, I suggested that her mother simply didn't like girls. Her answer made me sad.

"She didn't like *me*," clarified Maude, who thought it only fair to mention that Ethel had brought her sister's children—three boys and three girls—to the US from Canada when her sister died. Apparently all the children behaved badly; but Maude said her mother still favored the boys.

"I grew up knowing I could never be equal to my brothers in my mother's eyes," said Maude. "No matter how bad they were, I could never compare to how wonderful she thought they were. So I spent a lot of time trying to be as good."

Then she tilted her head and seemed to gaze at something far beyond the room we sat in that day. "Looking back now, I can see the things that were always good about me," said Maude. "I tried to be a good and honest person. I cared about what happened to others. I was very good at drawing, and did well in my jobs."

Maude took a sip of coffee, then set the cup down gently before adding, "I know it's sometimes hard to see this when you're young, but I finally learned that if you're comparing yourself to someone else and feeling bad about it, it's best to stop looking at others." Turning to face me, Maude said, "Find what's good about you and focus on those things."

Did she know I struggled with that? I was sitting with a woman who had spent nearly seven decades coming to that conclusion—now Maude's serenity was contagious. For a heart in turmoil like my own, her words and demeanor represented more than a point of view. They gave me hope.

I've always believed that if I get to know people well enough—and they begin to trust me—I'll see their brilliance. This has served me well as a teacher, in the corporate world, and as a writer. Maude's particular brand began to emerge as she told me about her educational and work experience, beginning with her entry into kindergarten. She hadn't been able to attend until she was six.

"The school wouldn't allow my father to enroll me in first grade without a name," Maude explained. "So he named me after his wife—Ethel Maude. I think he did it to spite her."

As I tried to imagine how it might feel to be the only child around without a name, Maude added, "I wasn't christened until I was eight years old."

Then she glanced away and chuckled at a memory of how her brothers had decided to call her Maude based on a cartoon about a mule with that name. "They thought they were teasing me but I was glad they called me Maude—at least I had a name," she explained.

Many years later, as I listened to that story again on tape, I remembered how my six-year-old brother's attempts to humiliate me were foiled every time he won another game of Old Maid by making sure I wound up with the losing card. "I got the Old Maid!" I would exclaim, jumping up and down with glee. To his eternal frustration, he never could convince me—at least not at age four—to feel bad about losing.

Fifteen years after Maude told that story about her brothers, I would see the humor. But in 2002, I felt anger and resentment as

I listened to her talk about boys who held all the power. On the job, I had been harassed by men within two different well-known and highly respected organizations by the time I was forty-five. My experience at the first company had taught me not to report what happened at the second—I believed it would damage my career. At home, I remained silently resentful about supporting the family while my partner spent the summer writing.

Apparently, and in spite of my feminist convictions, I still had a hard time speaking up on my own behalf. Only after leaving my marriage for good, going back into therapy, learning how to meditate, and finding a healthy partner would I remember the childhood card game with my brother and smile. I may have been physically small, but I had unwittingly thwarted my poor brother's attempts to make me feel small.

Listening again to the tapes of those conversations with Maude I heard myself ask, "Are there other things you can remember that shaped you?"

"I think having to do things on my own," began Maude. "I had to wash dishes and dry them; I had to wait on my brothers during dinner—they were perfect angels at the table. As for my clothes, I made them," recalled Maude, who said she also did her own washing and ironing by the time she was fourteen. "I don't begrudge that at all," she added. "That's the way it was in those days."

"You gained a lot of good skills," I said.

As Maude reminisced, I thought about how much I hated housework—doing dishes in particular. Then she paused, and when I looked up I saw her face brighten.

"But I loved everything about school," she continued. "Being with other kids, and the teachers . . . the teachers were so kind to me."

I was relieved to hear about this happier spot in Maude's childhood, which had begun to sound rather bleak. It was good to see her smile as she remembered how she had thought of school as "home," and described how the teachers encouraged her to pursue her artistic abilities in class. Suddenly, Maude's expression changed again.

"Recently, I was reading that in order to establish something you really love to do you need encouragement," she said softly. "And I started to cry . . . because I never got encouragement at home. There was never any talk of, 'What do you want to do when you get out of school?'"

I assumed there was no talk about her dream of being an architect, either—a dream that died when Maude wasn't allowed into the same class with the boys.

But Maude wasn't a quitter, so after high school she enrolled in design school. "I wasn't pushy enough," she explained, when I asked her why she didn't complete the program.

Fortunately, Maude's talent for technical drawing was finally recognized a year after she finished high school, when the Board of Education invited her to take a test that landed her a job drawing switchgears at General Electric. Somehow, in spite of her struggles at home, Maude had enough confidence in her math and drawing abilities to venture into nontraditional work settings.

"I worked with a group of engineers who would hand me specs of what they wanted and I would draw a picture of it," explained Maude. "Everything had to be right."

"Did you like it?" I asked.

"I loved being a drafter," answered Maude, who said she moved on two years later to the Philadelphia Navy Yard. "My father was employed there as a master shipbuilder—we worked on English ships that came in with sides that had been blown off," remembered Maude, explaining how she would draw the repairs needed according to the specs she received from the shipbuilders.

Was it unusual for women to be working in that field?

"Yes, it was, but they needed us because of the war rumblings. Hitler had taken over several countries by that time. At one point

I was asked to take a job for the State of Washington Navy Yard. They needed me up there and I was to be an example," she explained.

"So why didn't you take it?"

"I got nothing but flak from my brothers and their wives," replied Maude. "According to them, I was a slut if I went to Washington alone. And my father was not well—he had hurt his foot badly on the job and never did recover."

As I sat fuming about how unfair that was, Maude told me that when Jules's injury and lengthy hospital stay left her without his protection from the woman she routinely referred to as her "so-called mother," she knew she had to leave.

The first time Maude used it, I interpreted the term "so-called mother" to mean a mother who lacked parenting skills. At some point I knew I would ask about it, but at the moment I didn't want to interrupt her story. "You weren't a respectable woman if you moved out on your own because it would be assumed that you were making plans to live with a man," said Maude. "And to be respectable, you had to marry *before* he moved in." A few seconds later her voice dropped to nearly a whisper as she studied her folded hands on the table. "That was a terrible time for me—a time when more than once I thought about ending my life."

As I watched Maude's face, I thought of the relationships I enjoyed with my siblings—we'd certainly had to work through painful issues, even as adults, but those problems had only served to bring us closer. I couldn't imagine growing up without my mother's love and acceptance; my sister's companionship and collusion; or the support I could depend on from my brothers, whether or not they had liked me at any given moment. My father may have been opinionated, but he was 100 percent reliable as provider and head of the family. Of course, any one of my family members was capable of judging me in ways I perceived to be wrong or unwarranted, but in the end they always came down on my side.

I wondered what had kept Maude going.

Ironically, it was another taunt that reawakened the independence Maude had developed as a child.

"When my sister-in-law made a smart-aleck remark about how girls who enlisted were all whores, I finally pushed back and surprised even myself," explained Maude. "I said, 'I'm sorry you feel that way, because I'm going to enlist in the Navy.' I hadn't really thought about it until that moment, but for some reason I wanted to prove that I could do it."

While the Navy turned Maude down for being "too skinny," she was eventually accepted into the Women's Army Corps. Maude said she loved every minute of it.

"You know, leaving home at age twenty-two and enlisting took a lot of guts," I said, reflecting on my own lack of maturity at that age.

"I did have a lot of guts," agreed Maude. "I didn't know fear."

All morning, as Maude talked, I had forced myself to try and feel compassion for the mean-spirited players in her life. Having lived within a dysfunctional marriage myself, I knew firsthand how families could be ravaged by the effects of alcohol; I understood why children growing up with adults who drank too much often had to defend their parents' actions in order to survive. Throughout our interview I had wondered silently how Maude had been able to cope. But when she described, once again, how her "so-called mother" sometimes struck her across the head and face in anger, I finally had to ask how she endured that level of cruelty.

The answer lay in her relationship with her favorite aunt.

"Thank goodness for Addie," sighed Maude, referring to Ethel's older sister, a feisty RN who had served in Paris during World War I. "Adelaide rented a room in our house when I was small, and she would often tuck me into bed with her when she came off twelve-hour nursing duty," remembered Maude. "Even after she moved away she always made time to help when things got bad for me at home.

"Compared to Addie, my so-called mother was not a happy person," continued Maude. "Ethel didn't have a sense of humor," she added, shaking her head. "In fact, my Aunt Lizzie—the oldest sister—wanted to adopt me, but my father wouldn't hear of it. Unfortunately, Ethel seemed to hate every minute of her job raising me."

There it was again: "my so-called mother." For a few moments I had a hard time paying attention to what Maude was saying as I wondered what might be behind that label. I could understand why Maude would question Ethel's competence as a parent, especially in light of the physical abuse. But I wasn't sure why she would use her mother's first name rather than "Mom" or even "my mother."

According to Maude, mother and daughter were rarely together during the early years of Maude's life. Meanwhile, Addie lived as physically close to Maude as she could and was often called upon to protect her niece. "My parents would have these terrible arguments—mother would be screaming and throwing dishes—and I would be sent during the middle of the night to stay with my Aunt Addie," said Maude.

Confusing as those times must have been for Maude, they provided her with short periods away from the chaos. "I knew that someone besides my father cared about me. When you think about it, my aunt must have been very devoted. As I grew up, it was Addie who paid for my schools, and Addie who made sure I was prepared to support myself." Clearly, Addie was a strong role model, and perhaps even served as a parent figure for Maude, whose other aunts seemed to step in as well. But I was getting the idea that Maude had longed for a mother more like Addie, and had perhaps even thought of Addie as her second mom.

Unfortunately, the older Maude got, the less she and Addie saw each other. "She married a very nice, very handsome man when I was a teenager. I liked him a lot. But Ethel hated him and made it difficult for Addie and me to see each other. Of course, we remained in contact right up until she died, but we weren't as close as I wish we had been."

After Addie married and moved on with her life, the relentless conflict between Ethel and Jules continued to threaten Maude's safety.

"My father never argued with Ethel or fought back, but he would leave the house and stay outside walking all day," recalled Maude. "My brother and I would hide behind the sofa because Ethel would be throwing dishes in the kitchen. Eventually, my father would come back, but not until after dark."

Maude also recalled an image of her Aunt Lizzie chasing Ethel around the table, although she never knew what was wrong or what happened. That meant the fighting extended beyond Maude's parents. And I knew from my work with abused and neglected teenagers that children who see violence often play it out in their own adult relationships. *How did it play out in Maude's?* I wondered.

Meanwhile, Maude mentioned that Ethel eventually destroyed all the things her father loved—especially his music.

"You mean physically destroyed?"

"Yes," answered Maude. "She broke all his records, the phonograph . . . I don't know why he stayed with her. She had some kind of controlling influence over him."

Scary as that was, Maude said the loneliness was worse. "I had a book called *English Orphans*," she recalled at one point. "I thought of myself as an orphan and believed I just had to accept that was the way things were." Orphaned, but supported both emotionally and financially by Aunt Addie. This was when I truly began to suspect that Maude was building up to something significant—perhaps a painful memory she couldn't tell me about until she was sure I could be trusted. But I didn't want to influence what she remembered, or push her to speak of something she wasn't ready to discuss. So I waited. And finally, during my second trip to Ocean City, Maude decided to share what she had come to believe about her Aunt Addie.

MAUDE SAID IT was sometime before 1920 that Ethel Curley and her sister, Adelaide, had at separate times emigrated from England to the US.

"Their oldest sister, Elizabeth, came first from England," explained Maude. "Lizzie's boyfriend was here in the US, and he had a house and a wonderful job, so he sent for her." Maude smiled happily before adding, "I adored Lizzie."

Lizzie worked at home after arriving in the US. Eventually she sent for Addie, who came to work as a nursemaid. Last to come was Ethel, who also found a job working as a chambermaid.

"Ethel worked for the Bromleys, the family that owned the Quaker Lace Tablecloth factory and lived at the end of a trolley line. My father had a job turning the trolley around every day. He did that job because he had consumption and the doctors told him he had to be in the fresh air as much as possible."

That trolley line was where Maude's parents met, and soon Jules and Ethel were married. But according to Maude, Ethel wasn't an easy woman to live with—the youngest of several siblings, Ethel had been a young girl and still living at home when her mother died of cancer. Maude figured Ethel's father and older sister had overindulged her, to compensate for the loss.

"So she was spoiled," I said, using a term I hated personally but knew Maude's generation seemed to prefer.

Maude nodded her head in confirmation, adding that Ethel became "demanding and humorless" as a wife—traits that worsened as she medicated herself with alcohol. Maude believed it was during this time that her unhappy father turned to Addie.

"It must have happened in England," said Maude quietly. "By that time Addie was an RN and my father had enlisted in the military. Somehow, they wound up back in England together, and that must have been where Addie got pregnant—with me."

"You're saying your father had an affair with your aunt."

Maude nodded, adding that she was always told "Aunt Addie" had been forced to come home after being wounded during her service in Paris. Later, Maude came to believe Addie returned home to have a baby—a daughter Jules insisted he be able to raise in his own home. For Maude, evidence that Addie could be her biological mother must have felt like more than just getting her wish. It must have felt like a dream come true.

By the time we finally talked about it, I had all but guessed Maude's secret. When I heard the words come out of her mouth, however, I was shocked into silence as I placed my hand over Maude's. Our interview was over for the day.

Months later, I thought about how those long-ago decisions might have affected the individuals within Maude's remarkable story. I wanted to understand what might have motivated each character, so I tried to imagine what each of them had faced.

Take Addie, for instance. She would have felt horrible about falling in love with her sister's husband, and then acting on it. Once pregnant, she had had to choose between keeping the child—which would mean sacrificing her career and her reputation—and delivering the baby in secret. She would also have had to change the birth certificate. Once she turned her infant over to Ethel—the woman she betrayed—she would have watched in horror as her sister leveraged her rage by neglecting and abusing the child. Addie must have wondered, over and over, whether it would be better to simply take the child and live as an outcast. But then Maude would never see her father or know a family. She would be openly regarded as an illegitimate child. So Addie chose to watch from a distance, protecting when she could, and providing in less obvious ways. Her heart broken, she would have had to contain her anger toward a misogynist culture.

And then Maude herself, that child. Here was a little girl who grew up wondering what she was—or what she'd done—to provoke such cruelty. Hiding from her mother's rage, she blamed herself for Ethel's hatred. At the same time, Maude resented how her brothers were more loved, more indulged and entitled than she, in spite of their cruel behaviors. She must have lived for moments alone with her father and recovered—at least a little—whenever she spent time with the aunt who truly loved her.

And Jules, her father. Determined to right the wrong, he chose to raise his daughter under his own roof. To avoid shaming his family, he had asked—or perhaps even expected—his wife to parent a child who became for Ethel a constant reminder of her husband's infidelity. Caring for Maude when he could and protecting her when necessary, Jules watched his daughter pay both physically and emotionally for her parents' adultery.

But of course, there was one more critical player.

I could only imagine being Ethel, the wife whose husband had cheated with a woman who carried his child. Worse yet, the "other woman" was her sister, which would make the child her biological niece or nephew. How painful would *that* be? In spite of the humiliation—and to preserve her family's name and reputation—she had agreed to raise their child as one of her own, numbing feelings of anger and betrayal with alcohol. She was already caring for a five-year-old whose medical needs put financial, emotional, and physical strain on her marriage. Suddenly her caregiving duties doubled when she received an infant—a child whose very existence served as a painful reminder of her failure as a wife.

When did Ethel find out about the baby? I wondered. *How much time did she have to get used to the idea? Could any marriage survive that kind of pressure? And how would Ethel ever be able to reconcile her sister's actions—or forgive her for them?*

It would take more than a decade for me to see how quickly I had been willing to vilify the alcoholic parent—a woman with the same disease I was reacting to within my own marriage. Ethel's cruelty to Maude was well known, but what was the other side of the story?

I would never have access to those details, but I knew enough about alcoholism to guess. I knew it would have taken two people to create and maintain a toxic relationship that lasted that long. I also suspected Jules may not have had the courage to confront his wife about her drinking problem, opting instead to distract himself by having an affair. And where was Jules when his daughter was wandering around a city neighborhood at two o'clock in the morning? Surely he had participated regularly in the revelry that took him and his wife away from their duties as parents. Perhaps he had a drinking problem himself. Based on my belief that addiction is a response to physical or emotional pain, I wondered what else Ethel may have been facing.

Of course, these are not questions I would ever have brought up with Maude. I was amazed enough that she had survived her childhood with Ethel; I didn't need to open old wounds by questioning her father's behavior as well. Instead, I wanted to concentrate on the remarkable woman she had become.

"I THOUGHT WE'D have a salad tonight," said Maude one evening, as she walked from the table we used for interviewing toward her small but efficient kitchen. A clear plastic pitcher stood on the table, water trickling through the filter just beneath its lid. Every other surface in the room was clear of objects, and all were sparkling clean.

I watched as Maude removed one package after another from the refrigerator: lettuce, grapes, celery, walnuts, onions, carrots, and apples, each ingredient tucked into its own container. Then, with careful, precise movements, she began her work at the cutting board.

This must be how she performed her drafting work, I thought as

I watched Maude approach each item deliberately, methodically.

First she sliced half a head of lettuce into eight narrow pieces, then cut across each slice every half an inch until she had nearly filled a medium-sized bowl with the tiny pieces. Next, each of the dozen grapes she had carefully chosen were quartered and tossed into the bowl; a stalk of celery, cut into half-inch pieces, followed close behind. Fascinated, I continued to watch Maude's hands as walnuts and apples were chopped, onions minced, and carrots grated.

"I've never made a salad like this," I confessed.

"Well," replied Maude, "you can put just about anything you have into a salad if you cut it up small enough."

And if you have enough patience to do it, I thought.

"I didn't always have this kind of patience," said Maude, reading my mind. "It's one of the nice things about getting older."

As I watched Maude make our dinner, I considered what she had told me about her life, which included decades of days and months and years, all jumbled together like the colors of the salad she was assembling. Given the chaos of her first twenty years, I wondered how she had grown to be so cheerful. Maybe she had managed her emotions by doing tasks with tiny steps.

Personally, I had always felt frustrated by tasks that required tiny, repetitive steps—projects like making salad, doing needlepoint, or knitting even a short winter scarf. Yet I liked watching Maude, whose small, confident movements seemed calming somehow, almost hypnotic.

One evening, long after returning from my visit to Ocean City, I thought about Maude and decided to make that salad. As I cut and sliced and chopped my way through a slightly different blend of ingredients, I tried to consciously set aside my usual impatience so that I could engross myself in the task.

So far, so good, I thought after a few minutes, tossing a piece of jicama into my mouth. And that's when I realized I actually felt proud of myself for being able to work my way through such a labor-intensive salad. *Maude might be proud of me, too.*

A moment later I sensed a presence behind me—I knew she couldn't be there in the flesh, but it felt like Maude was looking over my shoulder.

"Just don't expect me to enjoy doing dishes," I said aloud, without turning to see whether her apparition was truly there. "Ain't gonna happen," I added as I imagined my friend smiling and shaking her head in amusement.

THE DAY BEFORE I left Ocean City, Maude told me what it was like to serve in a WAC detachment connected to the Army Air Corps. WAC was the acronym for the Women's Army Corps, which until 1943 had been known as the Women's Army Auxiliary Corps. Starting out in the state of Washington, Maude had signed up to do aeronautical engineering and worked with three other artists—all male—to create display boards used for training.

"I loved using my artistic abilities," remembered Maude, who believed her time in the WAC forced her to grow up. "I learned how to get along with people and make my own way as an adult."

The military would give Maude more than a chance to grow up—she was about to meet a man who would try, with some difficulty, to win her hand. Bill Kelly was a Master Sergeant based in San Francisco, where Maude had landed as well. "One of my girlfriends begged me to go with her and her boyfriend and Bill on a double date. I didn't want to go, but finally I gave in." At first Bill and Maude were good friends. "I wasn't all that interested," claimed Maude.

But when she moved back to Philadelphia, Bill was persistent. And things hadn't changed for Maude at home or at work, where only men remained in the drafting department of the Naval Shipyard. Surrounded by a chorus of male voices telling her to "Go home, girlie," Maude gave up on the shipyard and found a different drafting job. But correcting blueprints on yet another all-male team wasn't Maude's "cup of tea," and Bill was calling every night. So when he insisted on coming to Philadelphia to meet her family, she agreed.

"After that visit I realized I wanted to join him. I was falling for this guy," remembered Maude. "Besides, things were just different."

I thought about how a man like Bill might have appealed to Maude—someone who could take her away from the chaos and disapprobation she experienced at home. When I pushed for details, Maude said she had finally distanced herself enough from the opinions of her family to believe in her right to make choices for herself. She also felt that as an engaged woman she could finally leave town and not have to worry about being seen as a bad girl. So she took a train to San Francisco and married Bill the next week. When they discovered that the base chapel wasn't available, they had the ceremony in a friend's house, with only a few people in attendance. The next day Bill went back to work.

But none of that mattered much to Maude. Marriage had given her the permission she needed to move with Bill into a house on base. And when their house quickly turned into "party time," Maude used her status as Bill's wife to insist that they move to an apartment off base. Maude had told me more than once about her husband's penchant for partying, a habit that years earlier had driven Bill's father to yank his son out of college and force him into the service.

This was the point in our interviews when I began to wonder what role alcohol may have played in Maude's adult life. I knew better than to believe the problem had been resolved after a single intervention. At the moment, however, I was more interested in hearing how Maude had felt about Bill. Was she in love with him?

"Yes, I was," said Maude. "I realized that you become good friends before you actually fall in love with someone. And being around Bill as much as I was made me realize he was a great guy.

I was very happy." She also knew what to expect from a military marriage—the Air Force would always come first.

"Bill was a master sergeant overseeing most of the office work in the whole building," explained Maude, who described her husband as a "take charge" kind of guy who knew when he was right but was never nasty about it. I wasn't surprised to hear that Maude appreciated her husband's confidence. I did feel surprised by how easy it was for Maude to give up her career.

Silently, I ticked off what I considered to be the list of losses: income, financial and emotional independence, social status, and, most significant in my mind, self-respect. It wasn't until I listened to our recorded interviews many years later that I remembered—and was struck by—my own early job history. How could I have forgotten the deferential choices I myself had made in my twenties? I also sensed I had something to learn from Maude, so I forced myself to listen without judgment as she explained her decision.

"Bill enjoyed coming home to his wife, and I enjoyed cooking," replied Maude when I asked how it felt to give up her career. "We moved off base into the town, and it was just delightful to walk around and meet people."

It must not have felt bad to her, I admitted to myself.

Unfortunately, being a military wife required moving often. And while Maude accepted what that would mean, the multiple transfers eventually took a toll on the couple's personal life. "I didn't mind relocating," explained Maude as she listed the many places she and Bill had lived. "But after a while, when I wasn't able to get pregnant, my doctor said he thought moving so often was affecting my ability to conceive." So for a short while Bill left the military and moved with Maude to Illinois, to work for his father's business. Within a year, Maude was pregnant.

BORN IN 1951, Maude's curly-topped daughter Beth was a calm

and happy child. Three years later, Bill Jr. arrived, born with facial abnormalities that would require multiple surgeries. No stranger to the kind of care her son would need, Maude now devoted her time and energy to nurturing her family as they dealt with Billy's operations and recoveries. In that way, Maude's life was a lot like Ethel's had been.

During this period, Bill Sr. was back in the military, so the family continued to move—from Pennsylvania to Missouri and then back east again to Westover, Massachusetts, where they lived for several years. As her son reached adolescence, his medical needs no longer required Maude's full attention, but by this time other family needs defined her life. When I found out what they were, I was surprised.

Despite her conflicted feelings about Ethel, Maude felt responsible for her mother's care and began to travel regularly between Westover and Ethel's house in Philadelphia. At home Maude fought to maintain equilibrium as her husband, now in his fifties, struggled with high blood pressure and financial instability. At age forty-four, Bill had chosen early retirement over reporting for "advisor duty" in Vietnam. Later, I would learn that when Bill served in WWII as a twenty-four-year-old, he was sent ashore without a gun during the second landing at Iwo Jima. Twenty years later, he had had enough of war.

Instead, he moved his family repeatedly—four times within a few years—between Ocean City and Westover, to live rent-free in Ethel's three-story house. And each time Maude acquiesced, in spite of her own apprehension and exhaustion. At one point during our conversation, I asked Maude about the "exhaustion" she had mentioned experiencing at different times during her life. Was it physical? Psychological? I knew plenty of people who used that word to describe feeling emotionally overwhelmed by circumstances that seemed to be related to childhood experiences. So I wasn't surprised when Maude mentioned her lifelong quest for perfection.

"When I was young I tried so hard to get ahead . . . to be perfect, which meant being better than the next person," began Maude. "Later, when I became a parent, being perfect meant having a perfectly clean house."

Still looks pretty perfect to me, I thought as I looked around Maude's spotless apartment.

"But when you think about it, the amount of dust on the table isn't very important," continued Maude. "I know it *seems* important—especially in your thirties, at the apex of your life—but we can't be the best at everything. We can't change who we are, so we might as well accept what we actually do and who we are, and find more time for play. When I remember to do that, I always think, 'What am I so upset about?'"

Unfortunately, Maude came down with pneumonia right around the time Bill learned that his pension would not support his family. That's when he left the military for good and moved his wife and children, one last time, into the second floor of Ethel's house in Ocean City. When Maude told me about that decision I wondered, once again, how Bill's drinking might have affected his employment, the number of times he moved his family, and his ultimate decision to live with a mother-in-law who didn't seem to love or respect her daughter. But Maude had never identified Bill's drinking as a problem, and I didn't have the courage to ask about it. Years later, after my own marriage fell apart, I pondered why it would have been so hard to talk with Maude about a problem that had been so prevalent in my own life. I was a writer, after all, and had recently left a corporate communications job that had required me to ask far more difficult questions of people at the highest levels. But Maude's story hit close to home, and I hadn't been ready to admit to that.

Maude sometimes talked about being too afraid to speak . . . that hit close to home, too. Sometimes, in front of a group, I had experienced such intense stage fright that I would become verbally paralyzed and unable to breathe. I was good at helping other people—and in this case other women—find their voices. But there had been many painful moments during my life when I literally had no words. Moments when I lost my voice. At age forty-six, I wanted it back—somehow, talking to Maude was helping me figure out where and when I had lost it.

At the moment, Maude was telling me about how she had found herself living once again in the shadow of what she called Ethel's "hatred." And once again, the bright spot had been Addie, who had moved back to Ocean City after her husband died. She'd continued to love and care for the woman she believed to be her real mother, even as Addie aged and slipped into dementia. Maude also said she was the one among her relatives who found a nursing home for Addie when her aunt could no longer care for herself. And she remembered visiting Addie daily until her aunt died of cancer.

"The last time I saw Addie, she said to me, 'Oh, Maudie, I should have done things differently,'" Maude remembered. "I wish I would have said, 'You are my mother, aren't you?' . . . but I didn't, and then she was gone." Addie was eighty-seven when she died.

~

THAT STORY LED to a conversation about communication, a topic that had come up several times in our conversations.

"Even though my own family experiences weren't that good, I believe we need to communicate openly, beginning with our children," began Maude, who was more than ready to offer advice about this topic. "Start talking to your family as soon as possible, because open communication is a joy. It wasn't done in my time, but I know now that especially within a marriage, you have to open up and talk things over—it's important to take time to talk through misunderstandings. Ask what the matter is if you don't know . . . don't be afraid, because it always helps. Being open saves marriages as well as friendships."

What am I missing? I wondered, as I thought about the communication challenges within my own household. As I would come to learn, the effects of alcohol and the difference between "talking" and "open communication" would plague my relationships until I understood that waiting for my turn to talk during a difficult conversation was not the same as listening to the other person in order to gain understanding.

Meanwhile, Maude continued describing her recollections about another memorable period in her life. When Ethel died at age eighty-three—a few years after Addie passed away—her two sons sold the house and split the estate among all three children. Bill and Maude were both working at the time and didn't want to assume a mortgage. Instead, with their children grown and both "mothers" gone, they found an Ocean City apartment. "It was a lovely place," remembered Maude, who enjoyed the next two and a half years of calm.

But calm became chaos on Christmas Day in 1978, when Bill suffered a massive stroke. And from that day until Bill died of a second stroke nearly five and a half years later, Maude's life revolved around caring for her husband.

Living with a hemiplegic was all-consuming for Maude, but saying goodbye to her partner of forty-seven years was even harder.

"I was okay until about six months after he died," remembered Maude. "I had decided to go back to college and one night I simply fell apart while attending a class. I thought I had worked through every possible feeling, but I guess I hadn't. When I went to the doctor, he said I was badly undernourished . . . so I stopped going to school."

Here was a woman who had always loved school and finally had a chance to go, but now had to stop attending. It reminded me of my mother, who had gone back to school after her children left home, only to give it up when she thought others disapproved. And that made me mad.

Why, as women, do we do that? I thought. *Have we been trained to give up when something becomes difficult? Are we afraid to succeed?*

Meanwhile, Maude said she slowly pulled herself together by keeping busy—helping Beth put together an apartment and swimming three to four times per week. "It wasn't the sorrow that got to me," explained Maude, "it was feeling helpless after Bill was gone. I never really knew how much Bill had handled for the family . . . once he was gone I had to learn to do it all myself. I had to redefine myself as a single person."

I had begun to feel disappointed in Maude for dropping out of school—but the more she talked, the more I understood how learning to live independently after being married for nearly five decades would have been difficult for anyone, male or female. Maude's situation after losing Bill had required a different kind of education. Besides, how could I judge her for choosing to care for her physical needs?

"Women need to educate themselves about politics," said Maude when I asked about that. "I don't think we know enough about politics in this country, and the consequence is that we elect the wrong people into power." Maude uttered those words sometime between 2001 and 2005, but as I listened to the tapes in December 2016, her words were even more poignant.

"Personally, I don't think we have enough women in Washington," asserted Maude. "I'd like to see more women in power because they think differently than men. Women tend to be concerned about making children's lives better, and they tend to understand that you have to work for what you get."

I had agreed when she said it in person, and my mind hadn't changed more than a decade later.

ON OUR LAST day together, Maude spoke again of the transition she had been forced to make as a single woman. For example, she had learned how to handle her own money, an aspect of daily life from which married women of her era often abdicated. We hadn't talked much about money, but I could only imagine how it had played out at home during Maude's childhood. I'd always heard that sex, religion, money, and children were the issues couples used unconsciously to establish power within a relationship. Money—how and whether to save or spend it—had certainly posed enormous problems within my own marriage, so I imagined it could have been an issue for Maude as well. In her eighties, however, Maude was almost lighthearted about it.

"There are ways to make money work for you," she said matter-of-factly, "so if you don't know how to do it, learn as early in life as you can. You don't have to worship money to make it work for you."

Then she returned to the topic of independence. After Bill died, finding an apartment had been another challenge for Maude, who said she couldn't get away fast enough from the place she had shared with her husband.

"It held too many memories," she recalled, shaking her head. Her first experience with a new apartment and a dishonest landlord was difficult too. But eventually, that fiasco led Maude to the building she lived in during our interviews—a small, eight-story, HUD-subsidized residence for seniors.

"I've been here for over fifteen years, and my closest friends live right in my own building," said Maude.

During my last in-person visit with Maude, she told me she was dividing her time among her son and his family, who lived in Ocean City; her daughter, who traveled from Chicago when she could; and the friends who depended on her for rides to the grocery store and medical appointments. Maude seemed to have a rich and satisfying life.

"I'm eighty-two years old, so yes, I'm slowing down," admitted Maude on that last day. "But my life is full—I still take long walks along the beach and enjoy browsing through the shelves of my favorite bookstore two blocks away. Sure, I could feel sorry for myself and what I've been through, but why waste the time I have left?"

At that point our in-person conversation was nearing an end, but I had one more question for Maude—we had been talking about making choices, and I wanted her to comment on what she'd learned about setting priorities.

"These days we're consumed by trying to do everything all at once. We want to give 110 percent, but at my age you see how quickly time passes. And when we try to get everything done at once we lose ourselves . . . we're not kind to ourselves and sometimes that turns into not being kind to others. If you set priorities and give yourself a break once in a while, life is just more pleasant. You realize that getting everything done isn't what makes you happy."

This was a woman who had been very, very hard on herself—a person who had survived pain, loneliness, and loss throughout her life, and turned that life into something good by sharing it all with me. I felt honored to know Maude, and humbled by her words. I knew I would miss her when I left Ocean City, but didn't yet want to admit that it might be the last time we saw each other. So after a long, warm hug at Maude's front door, I told her that whenever I couldn't bear to say goodbye, I'd say "see you later" instead. And that's what I did before heading toward the elevator that would take me back to the parking lot. As I turned to wave one last time, I almost believed I'd be back.

ONE NIGHT SEVERAL years later, I stared at the frozen expanse of lake outside the window of a writing retreat I had rented for the winter and wondered whether I'd ever see Maude again. If I did, what would she look like? How might she have aged? I knew that since the last time we'd met, she had survived a serious illness. Her eyesight had surely deteriorated as well—would she be able to tell it was me? If I went to her apartment, would it be clean? Would she sleep a lot more than she used to?

That's when I realized I was afraid to find out. I was afraid to see what growing old did to people. Maude had seemed happy whenever I spoke with her, always emphasizing how much she enjoyed the freedom she had learned to give herself. During my second visit, when I had asked again about whether she feared the aging process, she'd told me she had long ago given up the notion of looking young. I thought about the photos I'd seen of Maude—images that clearly showed how she had changed as the years progressed.

When I looked in the mirror, I saw it was also happening to me. Unlike Maude, however, I couldn't stand to watch it.

Was that what I was trying to learn from these women? How to feel good about myself as I said goodbye to my youth? And then to middle age?

"No one wants to get older, but you can enjoy the process much more if you accept the limitations that come along with aging," Maude had said once over afternoon coffee. "It happened to me in my seventies, and it was a blow to my ego. But I got over it and now I just go with the flow. I don't dust every time guests come, but I am much better at not getting upset or excited. What I can't do just has to wait, and everyone is happier as a result."

And that's when it hit me: For Maude, the problem with aging had to do with what she could no longer *do*—not the way she looked. That was shocking to me somehow. *What about the way you look?* I wanted to scream. Maude looked fabulous for her age—FOR HER AGE. But who wants to get to that age in the first place? Who wants their skin to sag, their muscles to atrophy? Who wants their face to fall, and their balance to falter? At fifty-four I stayed in shape by dancing three times every week. At sixty I attended dance, yoga, and Zumba—and still the flesh swayed uselessly beneath both arms. I was disgusted.

Quite simply, I was furious about getting older. But in the company of the women I interviewed—every one of them—I seemed to be alone with my fears. Some even said they never thought about how they looked as they aged. They knew it was coming, and they accepted it.

Why couldn't I?

ONE DAY AS I sat with my dog, Mr. Magic, I realized it had been over a year since I'd spoken to Maude. So I decided to call her. Her voice was faint at first, but became stronger when she realized who it was on the other end.

I asked how she was doing and she started by telling me the details of her day. She'd been sick with something she couldn't quite remember the name of at the moment—but she seemed to have enjoyed the adventure.

"I've been in La-La Land," she said, and I could hear the smile in her voice.

"What do you mean, La-La Land?" I asked, intrigued. Although it occurred to me that Maude could be suffering from dementia, I told myself she probably wouldn't have been this aware of her confusion.

"Well, I did a lot of dreaming," began Maude. "I went somewhere else."

I thought that sounded like a side effect of medication and determined to ask Beth about it next time we connected.

"First, I was in the hospital for ten days," continued Maude. "Then I was moved to another place—can't remember what it's called—and the people who cared for us were so great."

Now I was starting to worry. Maude couldn't even remember what she had suffered from or where she had been and didn't seem to be concerned about it.

Later, she told me she spent a lot of time dreaming and claimed to know what "their" names were. That didn't make sense either, so when I asked who she was referring to, she said "they" were the characters she had been dreaming about.

Maybe my friend was having out-of-body experiences. Or communicating with spirits. Did she see them? Talk to them? Just as I was having images of Maude stumbling around her apartment in a nightgown, she told me that if she were smart she'd write a book about them.

With a sudden sense of clarity, I thought I understood what she was telling me. "Are you writing a novel, Maude? You could talk into a tape recorder," I said, trying to be helpful. I remembered how she had thanked me for helping her tell her story after our first visit in Ocean City. Later, I had sent her a red diary to encourage her to write. Now she was telling me her eyesight wasn't good enough to read anymore.

But Maude wasn't interested. "That's too much work; I'll leave the writing to you," she said.

SHORTLY AFTER THAT phone call with Maude, life as I knew it began to unravel and I set aside my work for several years. Once I felt sturdy enough to continue, I decided to reach out once more to Beth in search of Maude's phone number. I was thrilled to hear that Maude was still alive, but Beth warned me that her mother might not remember me. Diagnosed with progressive dementia, Maude was living in a nursing home. So I called my friend there.

"Hello, Maude," I said hopefully when I heard her cheerful voice on the other end of the phone. "This is Jenney Egertson—you may not remember me," I told her, speaking slowly, "but we spent some time together a few years ago. I interviewed you for a book I was writing."

And then she said something I'll never forget: "Well, I don't remember you, but I have the feeling we are very good friends."

Not *were* good friends. Or *have been* friends in the past. Present tense. And with that, my dear friend and I launched into the last wonderful conversation we would ever have in this world. Maude seemed happy with her life and where she lived, and as always spoke lovingly about her children and grandchildren. I told her about my daughter, described the work we had done together, and thanked her for the friendship and generosity she had shown me. I told her we had a lot in common. By the time we signed off I didn't even feel sad; instead, I felt grateful for the chance to reconnect one last time with a woman who had shared with the world her voice and her wisdom. A woman who had nurtured me on the path toward sharing mine.

THE NEXT FEW years went by quickly, so when I contacted Beth again in 2012, I wasn't surprised to hear that Maude had died two years earlier, after falling out of bed as she tried to get back home to Philadelphia.

"I'm sorry to say that she left this life in early August 2010," said Beth in a sweet email. Apparently, the dementia had progressed enough that Maude had to be moved from assisted living to the adjacent nursing facility, which she absolutely hated. Beth said her mother was so fixated on "going home to Philadelphia" that after about a month she fell out of bed while trying to do just that, and within a week succumbed to the injuries she had sustained.

That was not the image of Maude's final days that I wanted to be left with; I hated to think of my friend in pain. I didn't want to imagine her lying in bed with a broken hip, a black eye, or a dislocated shoulder. On the other hand, I was a tiny bit proud of Maude for being assertive enough to try and find her way home—in fact, that thought, and the image it evoked, made me smile. So that's the image I decided to stick with.

That day, feeling grateful that I had spoken with Maude while she was still happy, I tucked away Beth's email for a day in the future when I would finish her mother's chapter.

~

SIX AND A half years after Maude died, I would hear another version of her remarkable story.

"I'm wondering if Maude ever told you that she believed her mother, Ethel Hatman, was not her birth mother?" Beth wrote to me one autumn day, as we were corresponding about the tapes I had made of my interviews with Maude.

Of course, that "belief" lay at the very center of Maude's story.

Beth then described her search for documents, which included Maude's birth certificate and Ethel's immigration papers. Next came the news I hadn't wanted to hear: those documents proved Addie could not have been carrying a child on the day Maude's birth certificate indicated she had been born.

Beth also thought it was interesting that Maude never mentioned previous marriages she and Bill had each had before finding one another. My jaw dropped at that one. And she described a different and sadder version of her parents' relationship—one that included long periods of time when Bill had been stationed in places where his family couldn't join him.

At other times her parents' marriage was fraught with shouting and even nightly drinking, thereby providing the answer to my questions about whether Maude played out in adulthood the dysfunction she had been exposed to as a child. Beth also described the painful day she had overheard an uncle refer to her as Maude's "bastard daughter." Apparently, he was a devout Catholic who never recognized Bill's marriage to a Protestant as being legal. That would have hurt.

Maude's relationship with Addie included plenty of verbal fighting, too. And Beth had never heard of the "final" exchange Maude had described—the one in which Addie had said she wished she had done things differently. According to Beth, who kept close track of her great-aunt and visited her right up until the end, Addie had died alone at the County Home for the Aged in a vegetative, nonverbal state as a result of advanced dementia.

As I read through Beth's notes, I wondered whether she felt angry about her mother's fabrications, or the difficulties she herself had experienced as Maude's daughter. I could also hear the deep compassion she felt for her mother. As coauthor of a book about the significance of memories—whether true or false—Beth clearly respected her mother's stories.

Beth knew I would want to honor her mother's memories, but she also wanted me to have the facts. And that dichotomy was part of Maude's story.

BETH SAID IT was around 1976 when Maude began sharing her belief with family members that Aunt Addie was her birth mother. Apparently there was, for quite some time, just enough to what Maude said to make Beth wonder whether "suspension of disbelief was in order." However, in the process of working on the family history, Beth realized that what Maude believed would have been impossible.

Beth said she had been looking through papers in an effort to reconstruct the various addresses where her grandparents had lived after settling in Philadelphia, and one of them was Addie's citizenship naturalization document. Each time she read the document—and she did so several times—she set it down with "something niggling" at the back of her brain . . . something she couldn't identify. Then one day it simply leapt off the page: Adelaide Curley signed her naturalization certificate in an office of the Immigration Service—a public place—bringing with her two male friends as witnesses, on May 21, 1920. One day later, on May 22, 1920, Maude was born. At that time, no heavily pregnant woman would have been in public just a day before giving birth.

I had set that email aside for months, not wanting to deal with the conflicts it created within Maude's story. I didn't want the facts

Beth was presenting to be true. Why *couldn't* a woman have shown up at Immigration the day before she delivered a child? It wasn't illegal, was it? On the other hand, a professor of women's studies might know more than I did about that.

Later, I asked those questions of my friend Kate, who taught communications at the college level. "Pregnant women didn't go out in public in those days," she responded matter-of-factly. "There's no way a woman carrying a full-term baby would show up at Immigration."

Where does that leave me? I thought, feeling thoroughly discouraged. Did it mean I had to rewrite Maude's chapter? How could I choose her daughter's story over Maude's own recollection? There was only one thing to do: ask Maude. So I closed my eyes the way I did every day when I meditated, and I visualized Maude's face the way it looked when she was thinking about how to answer a difficult question. In my mind I saw her curious expression change slowly to a warm, encouraging smile.

Suddenly, I knew.

I NEVER MEANT to write an exposé—I didn't interview the women who entrusted me with their stories in order to reveal family secrets or champion my subjects' favorite causes. I did intend to honor what they told me, as long as it didn't harm the friends and family members who loved them.

I had certainly been angry on Maude's behalf as I wrote the first draft of her chapter, which championed *my* cause: to give Maude a voice after so many years of silence. But Maude had not been silent—before she died, her family had heard what she believed about her life and her parentage. And in the process of interviewing her, I had begun to exercise my own voice as well, and to question my anger toward men and the patriarchy I had felt imprisoned by for so many years. I was grateful to Maude for her help with my personal evolution.

There was no need to alter Maude's story—a sequence of events told in her own words that reflected some of her deepest feelings. In the end, most of us who make it to ninety will probably do so because of what we've told ourselves in order to survive. Maude told me what she *needed* to believe, in order to make sense of her childhood. The story she told me had become the truth for her, perhaps the only way she was finally able to find peace.

And that resourcefulness—that tenacity—is precisely what makes Maude remarkable. It's what I loved about her in life, and how I will remember her until the end of mine.

DRIVEN BY FAITH

Irene Egertson

I ALWAYS ADMIRED MY grandmother for her personal style and resourcefulness. In 1999, if you'd run into Irene at her favorite Minneapolis thrift store, you might have noticed her hat, the pin she'd made out of buttons, or perhaps the precision with which she had arranged her sleeves and collar that day. If she had spoken to you directly, you would have had to lean in close to communicate—at eighty-five, she didn't hear as well as she wanted to and complained about having less energy than she had enjoyed even at age eighty. But she loved conversation, with friends and strangers alike. And despite cultural directives from her church, her family, and society at large to keep her comments to herself, my grandmother spoke her mind.

She also knew it got her into trouble. During our interviews, Irene said she wished she could articulate opinions and explain her ideas more clearly. She worried about being too blunt, especially within her extended family, where her provocative comments and intrusive questions about religion, sex and marriage had become legendary. Her desire for acceptance was also well-understood. But her need to express herself always prevailed. And that tension—between the dictates of her generation to remain silent and the compulsion she felt to give voice to her thoughts—both plagued and defined this woman. My grandmother learned to follow the rules and survived by breaking them.

Hannah Irene, the fourth child born to Anna and Nils Egeberg, arrived on January 30, 1915. Late January wouldn't have been an easy time of year for a doctor on horseback to travel across the northernmost prairie of North Dakota, but it could have been among the most beautiful. On many winter mornings, the family's orange farmhouse and red barn stood in bright relief against a cold blue sky and frozen snow pack—an enduring childhood image for the artistic Irene, who remembered those days with great affection. "It was a large farm, 360 acres, with a big house and a huge barn filled with cattle and horses," recalled Grandma one morning as she gazed into her coffee cup. "We had five bedrooms, a large kitchen, a large living room—oh my, it was such a beautiful house."

I loved it when my grandmother talked about her happy memories of the farm. That day her face shone with joy when she described how she had used spare pieces of fabric to make doll clothes, and fashioned costumes for plays out of old lace curtains. She remembered with special fondness the winter rides to church in a "cutter"—a covered platform built on blades and pulled across the snow behind a team of horses.

"I remember black nights with clear skies and shining stars," sighed Grandma. "I'll never forget listening to the jingle of the horses' harnesses and the sound of their hooves breaking through the hard, crisp snow on the way to Christmas service."

Many of my grandmother's early memories also revolved around her mother—a slender, tallish woman known for gentleness, stamina, and piles of thick brown hair swept up into a bun on the top of her head. "My mother was the prettiest lady in the whole area," said Grandma. "Her hair was elegant, pulled up loosely with combs so that you could see the total beauty of her face." Grandma also explained that an attractive woman wouldn't have received compliments in those days—at least not from her family.

"Women worked hard," she told me. "My mother was busy from morning to night with cooking, cleaning, laundry, and caring for young children and babies . . . and she never criticized or complained." Anna didn't even complain when her husband—a pious, dogmatic Christian sixteen years her senior—demanded more children. After Irene's birth, and in spite of the wartime economy, four more babies arrived in rapid succession.

The feminist in me rebelled when I heard that. "Wow," I said aloud, imagining a young, heavily pregnant woman lugging buckets of water across a frozen yard while inside the house a baby screamed and older children watched their mother from an icy window. I figured that in those days a God-fearing man would regard the use of any kind of birth control as being sinful. But why would a logical person want to support more children during economically unstable times?

"I guess he wanted to be like Abraham from the Old Testament," explained Grandma. "Abraham's sons led the twelve tribes of Israel, and my father wanted to honor the Bible by being like Abraham."

I already felt plenty of anger about the pressures women across cultures have felt to produce children, whether or not it made sense. So when I asked my grandmother how she thought her mom felt about the prospect of bearing and caring for that many kids, she said Anna had managed well with three but that by the fourth child she had a hard time keeping up with housework.

I knew Irene also believed the fight for women's rights during the 1970s had burdened American women with too many choices, so I was surprised when she suddenly became quiet and then said, "Thinking back to my mother's time—believe it or not—women had ways of getting rid of the fetus."

I watched her face closely, preparing for an emotional tirade about how women who chose abortion would be damned forever. Her actual response was mild but powerful.

"And we did not know that was wrong," she said. "Isn't that strange?"

I sat in stunned silence, not entirely sure I understood what she meant. Did she believe that abortion had always been wrong and Christians during Anna's time simply hadn't figured it out yet? Or, was she saying that in Anna's day—and for good reason—abortion had not been considered to be wrong? I'm not sure I wanted to know, so when I was able to find my voice all I said was, "Yes, it is strange; the question now is, exactly who decided it was wrong, and why?"

Grandma merely shook her head as she looked down at the table.

Feeling emboldened, I kept on going. "In a lot of countries it's not wrong. In your mother's time, I'm sure thousands of women, including Christian women living in our own country, used those herbs to prevent their own deaths . . . and to prevent their other children from growing up without mothers."

"Back then men expected to keep the women pregnant," said my grandmother, looking up finally. "In our area we had a lot of families with twelve children. But in those families the older children took care of the smaller ones. And those women had loving husbands."

I understood she was comparing those marriages to her parents' troubled relationship, so I didn't comment. I also wondered whether Anna had resorted to using the herbs. But when Grandma didn't say more, we moved on.

MOST OF MY family had heard the general story about Irene's childhood, but I wanted details. So that morning, after we had caught up on family news, I sensed my grandmother might be ready to talk about the disturbing dynamics between her parents. I wanted to hear it in her words, finally.

"We didn't know much about World War I or the economy; we were like everyone else, and no one had money in those days," explained Grandma. "We'd turn an old crate into a table or cupboard when we played 'house,' and when it was time to play 'school' the crate became a desk."

When I suggested her father's rules about religion may have been a little harsh, Grandma said it wasn't about that, either, even though parameters on the Sabbath were especially strict. "You couldn't sew or even cut with a scissors," she explained. "On Sundays we couldn't play until we had listened to Father read devotions after lunch. While he was reading, and he always read in Norwegian, we had to be completely quiet."

I began to feel a little sheepish about my own childhood complaints around attending a two-hour service once a week.

"Of course it was hard," she continued, "but we didn't feel any different from other families. Lots of them were strict in those days." Then she paused before adding, "In our family we experienced a lot of bad things and also good things growing up, but in general we had a difficult time because Dad had a problem with Mother."

"What kind of a problem?" I asked. I couldn't imagine how the gentle, white-haired woman I had known growing up could be trouble for any man.

"Mother was unusually good and kind and tolerant and understanding," said Irene, avoiding the real question. "If it weren't for her, I don't know how we as children would have made it." I could tell that going into more detail would be painful for my grandmother, so I didn't probe. Later, however, she would admit that the criticism, jealousy, and physical blows Nils directed toward his wife had created intense fear and anxiety for her and her siblings.

The day of that particular interview I had wanted to ask how

Nils had expressed jealousy—especially since Grandma herself had problems with jealousy, and seemed to feel especially threatened by her husband's attentions to his daughters-in-law. I also wondered whether Irene and her siblings had been physically or sexually abused. But I knew without asking that Nils had been a man to be feared. And it was fear for her life and the well-being of her children that finally drove Anna to leave her marriage—a course of action that would forever shape Irene's personality and her view of the world.

In 1927, leaving a marriage would have been difficult for any woman, and especially for a mother with small children. To do it successfully, Anna Egeberg knew she would have to wait patiently for the perfect opportunity. Such an opportunity presented itself one cold April day, three months after Irene's twelfth birthday. Late that afternoon, the horses got out of the pasture, and Anna knew Nils would have to retrieve them. She also knew how long it would take—enough time to gather her children, get them into their coats, blow out the kitchen lamp, then hurry out the door to run a quarter-mile across plowed fields to the home of a neighbor.

"Mother barely got her coat on," recalled my grandmother. "And crossing the fields was very difficult for us children, but we made it to the Greens' house—mother and I, one sister, and my two-year-old brother. Mother had to pull him behind her on a sled." Anna's other son was helping Nils with the horses, and the four oldest girls were away at boarding school.

Irene's features darkened as she described that day in halting phrases. I imagined a woman trying not to stumble as she pulled the sled behind her with one hand and held up her heavy skirt with the other. Panic and determination played across her face as she encouraged her two daughters to hold hands and run as fast as they could across the icy fields. *What would have happened if Nils had caught them?* I wondered. *Or if Anna's neighbors had turned them away?*

Apparently, Anna hadn't taken a chance with her neighbors. "Mother was close to Amanda Green," recalled Grandma, "and Amanda's husband, Arnold, had worked for my dad." Anna also knew that Arnold disliked his former employer, and she correctly guessed that he would be more than willing to watch the fields in case Nils came after his family that day. But Nils didn't come, so when Arnold finished his chores, he piled Anna's family into the car and drove them to the home of Mrs. Sivertson, another neighbor who lived two miles away. Arnold knew without a doubt that within those walls Anna would be safe—even Nils wouldn't cross Mrs. Sivertson, a formidable Norwegian both feared and respected by the entire community. And Arnold was right. Nils didn't pursue his family until the next day; when he did, the matter was settled quickly. But according to Grandma, "It took a miracle."

"When Father called the house, Mrs. Sivertson said he could come over," remembered my grandmother. But Mrs. Sivertson promised nothing beyond that. By the time Nils arrived with his oldest son, Anna and her children were upstairs, huddled together behind a locked door.

Why would she let him even get near them? I wondered.

"When he got to the top of the stairs, my father called to Mother over and over, but Mother wouldn't answer," continued Grandma, who said Nils appealed to his younger son next. "He never scolded the boys, so we all thought our little brother would go with Dad," explained Grandma. "But Mother had my brother on her lap and began making a doll for him out of her handkerchief. He must have been distracted because he didn't utter a word." Finally, when faced with silence, Nils and his other son returned home.

After Grandma finished her story, we both sat quietly for several minutes. "Divine intervention," I said finally, hoping she wouldn't seize the opportunity to lecture me about my faith. Lucky for me, that wasn't a day for evangelizing; when I asked for additional details, my grandmother said the family returned to the farm after Nils agreed to certain conditions.

"Did he comply?" I asked, holding my breath.

"Well, the truce didn't last long," said Grandma. "One night when Mother stood at the stove, Dad shook his fist in her face for the last time." According to Grandma, events happened fast after that. Within a few days, Anna's brother Olaf arrived to take his sister back to their parents' farm in Minnesota. While the younger children stood together in their coats, Olaf asked Nils one last time for a promise not to scold Anna. "If she needs it, I will," replied Nils. That's all Olaf needed to hear. Even Anna's oldest son had had enough. "Papa, get my coat," he said. Without a word, Nils handed over the coat and watched his family walk out of his life.

IRENE EGERTSON LOVED her grandchildren passionately; she also liberally exercised her matriarchal role, which she believed gave her license to express her opinions about our lives and decisions forcefully and directly. Sometimes, when Grandma tossed a critical comment my way, I'd question whether she loved me at all. But the more I learned about her childhood, the easier it was to understand the basis for her pointed questions about my spiritual well-being. Perhaps she believed it was her job to monitor her family's spiritual practices—she may have learned that from her father. And her famous question, "Have you accepted Jesus as your Lord and Savior?" was surely informed by her strict evangelical upbringing.

Secretly, I admired Irene's courage—she wasn't afraid to challenge the authority figures in her life, be they senior pastors, high-ranking members of her congregation, or the male elders within her husband's family. While she often claimed to feel thwarted, those feelings didn't stop her from expressing her views, however clumsily. I wanted to understand this woman, and felt I had something to learn.

I also knew I was missing an important piece of her story—an event referred to by her children as "Irene's vision." She herself would mention it occasionally, but I never felt I had the right to pursue more information. So it was with great anticipation and some degree of trepidation that I turned on my tape recorder one blustery day in late winter to ask about this particular moment in my grandmother's life.

"I know you had a vision as a child," I began as I sipped a cup of the strong coffee we always drank at her house.

"Oh, I don't know that it was actually a vision," replied Grandma, dismissing the event. "I'm not even sure it happened."

"Well, something happened, because you've spoken of it often. You've said you saw Jesus," I countered, knowing how she loved to talk about her faith, hoping this would tease the story out of her.

It did.

After leaving the farm, Irene and two of her sisters had moved back to town with their grandmother. There, Irene made friends easily. Unfortunately, her social life ended abruptly the day she suddenly collapsed on the school playground. She barely remembered the incident, she admitted. "But I do recall being thrown over Olaf's shoulder. Then everything went black." The next thing Irene knew she was back at the farm, recovering from a dangerous case of encephalitis.

"When I woke up from the coma, my mother told me the doctor had not expected me to live. And being a religious person—even as a child I was a serious Christian who loved the church—I wanted to talk to Jesus about this." My grandmother's eyes lit up whenever she mentioned Jesus's name. "So one day I sat up in bed to pray and I asked Him, 'Why did you save my life?' When I opened my eyes, I thought I saw Jesus standing in the doorway. Then, in my mind, I heard Him say, 'Hannah, I have something important for you to do when you grow up.' That's all He said."

For some reason my grandmother had begun to downplay that event, even though her children and many of her grandchildren knew the story. I also knew she had never doubted, growing up, that she would know at some point exactly what her Savior wanted her to do.

Her family moved to Cyrus after leaving the farm. "I adjusted pretty quickly to my new home and remember being very happy," said Grandma, who also said she made friends easily and liked the boys. "At that age everybody giggled instead of talking," recalled Irene, who said her mother eventually found a large two-story house in Cyrus, located on the other side of the tracks. She smiled as she described the wintertime fun she and her siblings had sliding down the snow-covered hills without sleds, which they couldn't afford to buy. But her face fell suddenly when she talked about being confirmed, a spiritual milestone she had taken very seriously.

"I was sad because Mother didn't attend church," remembered Grandma. "But I also had a wonderful pastor who helped explain the way of salvation and God's love." When my grandmother told me she hadn't believed she should get confirmed because she wasn't sure she could keep the promise she would be required to take publicly, I was shocked. I knew she was serious about her faith, but this degree of consternation was something I could hardly imagine.

"I didn't understand that God would help me keep the oath," confessed Grandma, "so I felt very ashamed about that."

Why was she so hard on herself? I wondered. It had never occurred to me that the promise we all made at our confirmation ceremony could be that important to any teenager.

"The day of my confirmation, Mother had invited relatives to dinner," said Grandma, whose baptismal sponsor had taken a snapshot of Irene at home—most confirmands had a formal photo taken at church. "I was never sure why Mother didn't come to my confirmation, but I guess it was because she didn't go to church at all," said Irene.

I waited in silence for more.

"Maybe she was embarrassed because she had left her husband . . . that was kept a secret, but Mother may have thought of it as something that should never have happened."

I wondered if Grandma felt that way too. Taking on responsibility for a man's behavior was relevant to my own life and, in my opinion, an all-too-common response among women. If a man I was involved with became angry, it was my job to appease him, regardless of what he had done. If he got frustrated, I would look for ways to change my behaviors so that he felt better. If he wasn't getting enough attention, I assumed responsibility to accommodate his needs, however unreasonable. If my schedule didn't fit with his plans, I'd change mine. In my world, men didn't have to face their feelings or alter their behaviors. Instead, to prevent them from leaving, I would simply make things right.

That was still going on to some degree during the time I interviewed my grandmother, who believed she had accommodated my grandpa more than she should have. But she didn't feel that way about her own mother.

"No—I never felt guilt about Mom leaving Dad because I saw how he treated her," said my grandmother. "My dad was physically and verbally abusive, while Mother was God Herself to me."

"You must have felt relieved by your mother's actions," I suggested.

"What Mom did was brave and courageous," confirmed Grandma. "She probably saved her own life by leaving her husband. Dad wasn't mean to us kids, but he was cruel to Mother; my father had a problem with jealousy and he also had a temper."

I wasn't sure I believed that Nils wasn't cruel to his children—and if not Nils, I suspected someone else may have gotten to them, whether verbally, physically, or both. I understood that children who witness acts of violence between their parents can feel traumatized into adulthood, so I figured Irene's anxiety, her tendency to argue, her inability to gauge how her words might affect others, and some of her emotional outbursts could be explained by that. But Irene also exhibited unusual—sometimes even inappropriate—behaviors from time to time. And figuring out my grandma was important. I needed to find a good reason for Irene's mercurial nature—an explanation for her alternating displays of meanness and generosity. I wanted to understand her ability to be loving one minute and devastatingly critical the next. To be so accepting and tolerant socially, but narrow and rigid when it came to her family's spiritual lives.

I also defended my grandmother passionately whenever a family member referred to her as "dumb." Like many of the women in my extended family, I knew Irene retreated into silence when her husband gave her what she and her daughters-in-law called "the look"—a sudden, almost explosive expression of rage and disgust directed at whomever dared to disagree with an Egertson male. Only my beautiful aunt Vonnie—the oldest of Ernie's children and the one female who could control her brothers—escaped that look.

Finally, I understood, at least intellectually, that Grandma had been powerfully affected by her childhood, as well as the dynamics within her marriage. And I tried to remember those facts whenever she directed her disapprobation toward me personally. But even in my late forties I felt provoked by what I perceived to be my grandmother's religious zeal. While I had great respect for the drama she had experienced during her youth, it would take me another sixteen years to accept—and even appreciate—the bedrock of her faith and how it served her.

ONE EVENING, GRANDMA called to tell me she'd found the perfect rug for the living room in my tiny Arts and Crafts bungalow. Rushing over to her house, my daughter and I imagined an antique, rose-colored rug that would magically pull together years of impulse furniture-buying and wall-painting. But when Grandma dragged the rug out of her car trunk, Rowan shook her head and I got a stomachache.

Looking at it under the light in Irene's kitchen, I tried to imagine the rug's blue-green and orange floral pattern against the lime-green walls of my living room. Gently, I told my grandmother I didn't think it would work. Of course, I knew she wouldn't be happy, but I wasn't prepared for her response.

"Can't you just go home and try it?" she asked impatiently, her voice rising with each word. "Does a gift have to be perfect? Can't you try to work with a gift even if it's not perfect?"

"The rug is beautiful, Grandma," I said, pushing away images of the color clash ahead. "Buying the rug was a wonderful, thoughtful thing for you to do." But Grandma had no interest in what I thought was nice.

"I don't care what you think of what I did, I want you to like it," she countered. "But don't give it away; if you don't like the rug, bring it back and I'll use it in my TV room."

As soon as we got home, I put the rug down in our living room and Rowan agreed that it looked terrible. But when she proceeded to tell me what else looked terrible—the wall color, my $900 area rug, the new chair I had just bought—my brain overloaded. I was still gritting my teeth when the phone rang half an hour later. Those were the days when heavy plastic telephones hung from the walls or sat on desks. Thankful for the respite, I ran to the kitchen.

"Hello?" I answered, wondering who would be calling at that time of the evening.

"I just want you to be happy with your house," said the tearful voice on the other end of the line. It was my grandmother, and I could hear that her voice was shaking. "But I'm impatient."

"I am too, Grandma," I replied, admiring her courage. "And I know you just want to help."

"You can give the rug away," she whispered. "I love you."

"I love you too," I said. Then we both said it again.

When I heard her hang up, I paused to look out my kitchen window at the fading light. "Oh Grandma," I sighed as I reached for a napkin to wipe my nose. "Whatever will I do when you're gone?" Then, slowly, carefully, I hung up the phone, my own vision blurred with tears.

During Irene's childhood, money would have been scarce, especially for a single female trying to support eight children. So when three of Irene's older sisters finished high school and found jobs in Fargo, North Dakota, Anna and the rest of her family moved away from Cyrus to join them. The year Irene began ninth grade, she and her younger siblings found whatever work they could, washing dishes or babysitting outside the home.

Unfortunately, odd jobs weren't enough to keep a large family going, so Irene left public high school during the spring of her sophomore year to mop floors at a local hospital. Never resenting or questioning the interruption, she received her reward the next fall, when she learned she would complete her junior and senior years at Oak Grove Lutheran High, the boarding school her sisters had attended. Grandma never figured out how her mother came up with the tuition, but claimed those years at Oak Grove were among the happiest of her life.

"Your mother was always there for you, wasn't she?" I commented as my grandmother described those years. Her undying devotion to the woman I knew as my great-grandmother had always been clear, but now I understood why.

"Oh my, yes," said Irene. "She was so strong . . . so beautiful, even when her life was hard. She always helped me in any way she could."

That was certainly true after Irene graduated from high school and found herself living back at home—sullen, depressed, and unattached. Once again, Anna stepped in by sending her daughter to Minneapolis to live with an older sister, who was about to begin nurse's training. In those days, unmarried women became nurses, teachers, or secretaries, and Irene's sister had lived at home for seven years after high school. Determined to avoid that fate, Irene convinced a hospital administrator to hire her as an aide despite her lack of training. Although the work was physically taxing, Irene was popular.

This was a side of my grandmother I had never heard about—the young, independent woman who loved helping others. Not that she wasn't generous or loving in her later life, but my recollections of her over the years—images collected from family events and dinners we had attended together—were of a woman who often seemed nervous. A nervous person certainly wouldn't have been popular among old people, I thought. Maybe the Egertsons made her anxious.

"I loved caring for those people," continued Grandma. "And I did whatever it took to make them comfortable."

When I thought about how starved for conversation and purpose my grandmother must have felt while stuck at home in North Dakota, I could understand how being an aide might have brought out some of her best qualities as she grew into a young, independent woman. I wondered what it was like to be a single woman in the 1930s—she would have been twenty years old in 1935.

"Well, most young women got married," she began. "If you weren't married by age twenty-five, you were seen as an old maid." Then she used her mother as an example, filling in details I had wondered about for some time. "My mother's parents were really responsible for encouraging her to marry Dad because he was a Christian." She surprised me when she added, "The other guys my mother liked were not Christian, and her parents wanted to get her married before age twenty-five."

I remembered my great-grandmother as being quite

religious—perhaps even pious—but maybe that hadn't always been the case.

"My mother was very protected and extremely naïve, with no idea of how men behave during dates," explained Irene. "In fact, she was horrified by the thought, and my dad may have been the only available man Mother knew about—at least she never talked about dating anyone else."

Grandma had already told me that in those days dates meant going on a buggy ride; I also knew Anna was twenty-three and Nils was thirty-nine when they married. Maybe Nils had been considered to be a good catch: in 1900 he had gone to North Dakota and worked on a farm as a homesteader for five years before the government gave it to him. By the time he met Anna, the oldest of eight children, Nils needed a wife and his family lived close to hers.

"She was beautiful and he had his choice," said my grandmother. "Mother was already twenty-three, so she knew she'd better marry him."

Put yourself in Grandma's place, I instructed myself one day in late summer of 2017 as I reviewed those notes. As a child, the most influential man in your life is verbally, physically, and emotionally abusive toward the person you love and depend on most in the world: your mother. The other man you know well—your uncle—is caring, loving, available to help, and strong enough to stand up to his dangerously angry brother-in-law. That means good men exist. Your most important female role model does her best to support and care for her large family. She fights for your happiness, but in some way feels guilty about her own choices. What does a child take away from that environment?

I kept reading. Grandma had told me she was happy and outgoing in her twenties, with lots of friends.

"In Minneapolis, my social life revolved around church," she explained. "There were lots of boys there, and my dream was to get married and have kids. My boyfriends were Christian—I wouldn't date anyone else," remembered Grandma. "No one had money in those days, but we went out for rides and swam at lakes in groups. During the summer we would go water pedaling—riding in a chair that sits in the water—and in winter we always went skating."

During that time Irene also attended two Lutheran churches. "I went to Lutheran Brethren and also to St. Paul's Lutheran, where Rev. H.O. Egertson was pastor," she recalled. She also described how she would coordinate skating parties from both churches so that she could attend all of them. "I had lots of fun during those years. Church was the number one function in our lives, and I went to all the events—not because of religion, but because the boys were there," explained Grandma. "Guys were number one on girls' minds," she added, her expression becoming more serious. "We were all looking for the right person to fit our personalities—and there were a lot of nice men out there. In fact, there wasn't a bad one in the bunch."

"What were they like?" I asked.

"They were Christian, God-fearing men who lived for God and behaved themselves like men should behave," said Grandma with sudden conviction. "They followed the rules of their Judeo-Christian faith and kept them stringently."

And there we have it, I realized. *You thought that's who you were getting when you married a man who said he was Christian—a man outside your circle, but a Christian nevertheless.*

That man was Ernie Egertson, and I was looking forward to hearing the details of my grandparents' courtship. I knew Grandpa had lost the love of his life when his first wife died of eclampsia shortly after delivering my uncle, their fourth child. I wondered why a beautiful woman like Irene—who surely would have had other prospects—had taken on the enormous responsibility of marrying a man with four children.

"Ernie's older brother, your great-uncle H.O., was pastor of the Lutheran congregation where I went to church," my grandmother began. "I had vowed I would never marry a man with children, so when my pastor suggested I meet his brother, I had plenty of reservations."

But according to Grandma, something always seemed to happen to her resolve when it came to this slim, dark-haired Norwegian. On many weekends during their short courtship, Ernie would make the hundred-mile drive from Albert Lea to Minneapolis to visit Irene and spend time with his youngest son, who lived with his brother's family while my grandpa got back on his feet.

"Why did you get involved with him?" I asked my grandmother.

"Ernie was charming," admitted Irene.

"But he had four children and you had made a promise to yourself," I argued.

"That's right," she said. "And I knew I wasn't in love the day I agreed to marry him."

That stopped me cold. Did my grandparents not love each other?

"So that night," she continued, "remembering the promise I had made to myself, I decided to break the engagement."

I was willing to bet few, if any, people knew this part of the story.

"Then I remembered my vision. Could raising these children be the 'work' Jesus wanted me to do?"

One thing every person in Ernie Egertson's extended family knew for sure was that his wife, Irene, had believed she had been chosen by God to raise his children. This time, when my grandmother referred to her role as Jesus's "work," I revisited my feelings about that. On the one hand, I had begun to question exactly why my grandfather had chosen Irene—because his children needed a mother and his oldest brother thought she would be a good choice? That sounded unfair to Irene. But I wasn't feeling so great about her reason for marrying Ernie, either. After all, I had heard about and witnessed throughout my life the difficulties surrounding Irene's relationships with her children. I had also been both hurt and annoyed by what I considered to be Irene's religious fanaticism. Why had I decided to devote a chapter to Irene? Did I feel like I owed my family a spot in my book? Or was I ready to try to understand and perhaps even learn from someone whose faith had literally saved her life? Did I want that for myself? It certainly felt like I was ready to examine what made my grandmother tick. So I asked how she had finally made the decision to marry Grandpa.

"Well, I turned to Jesus," she said. "And when I prayed I said, 'If I am supposed to marry this man, please help me to love him.'"

I held my breath as Grandma looked down at her folded hands. Then she said, "The next time I saw Ernie, things were just different. I was falling in love." So she did love Grandpa. And that's when she accepted the job of raising Ernie's children. By the time Irene joined the family in December of 1939, less than a year after meeting Ernie, he was thirty-two and the children were nineteen months, six years, eight years, and thirteen years old. Irene was twenty four.

Suddenly I had switched to Grandma's side again. *The job of raising Ernie's children*, I said to myself as she finished her story. Here's a woman who had promised herself not to take on someone else's children. A fiancée who almost reverses her engagement because she doesn't love her suitor. Then she marries him anyway, to obey her Lord.

That raised some questions: Did my grandmother betray her own needs and desires to take on this nearly impossible task? Irene was used to backbreaking work, both at home growing up and at her job caring for the elderly. But she was stepping into a broken, grieving family.

I thought about my biological grandmother, Ernie's beloved first wife—the young mother who had died tragically because of an error on the part of the physician who misdiagnosed her eclampsia. Any new bride might feel initially insecure in a marriage to a widower who had deeply loved his first wife—a man whose in-laws had become his extended family when he moved in with them. But I knew these circumstances may have been especially difficult for Irene, whose jealous nature often interfered with her relationships.

I didn't need to ask my grandmother whether she felt like a bonafide member of the Egertson clan, either. Throughout my life I had watched Grandma lose control at family reunions and milestone birthdays when she stood up to talk about how desperately she wanted to feel accepted. Each time it happened, her grown children would attempt to console her while the rest of us observed in painful silence. I considered these outbursts to be a normal part of Egertson family events, so I wasn't surprised when Grandma would dissolve in tears before her audience; and I imagine I wasn't the only one who cringed each time she took center stage. I did, however, want to know what lay behind those feelings. Finally, as an adult, I had the courage to ask.

One day as we sat together at her kitchen table—a powerful symbol of safety and connection—I brought it up.

"I know stepping into the family wasn't easy for you. What was it like to raise children who had lost their mother?" I knew the situation had turned out to be far more difficult than Irene had anticipated.

"Before we were married, Ernie made so many promises about how we were going to live together, raise this family together, and teach them all the good things there are in a marriage. Then, all of a sudden they were gone," said my grandmother.

"What was gone?"

"The promises he made," answered Grandma. "I know I wasn't always patient, or able to express the kind of love the children needed. But when I would go to their father, wanting to consult about a problem with a child, his answer would be, 'Well, their mother didn't have any problems, she managed them just fine; you just don't know how to handle them."

"Ouch," I said, wincing. Did the sweet grandpa I knew all my life really say mean things like that to his wife?

Apparently, comments like that convinced my grandmother she wouldn't be getting any help from her husband. But she didn't have enough experience to parent Ernie's children on her own, and she lost their respect when she tried.

"The children would ask me for permission and I would give one answer . . . then they would go to their dad and he would have another answer. My rules and regulations for decisions had no effect on them that I could see," recalled Irene, who said the problems with her children also affected her marriage because she felt like she wasn't valued. Her view of herself changed as well.

"I had their respect before the marriage—I thought I was a gift from God," remembered Grandma. "I was going to take Ardis's place and do everything that she now couldn't do. I was so sure of that because I had God's promise. 'This is what I want you to do,' Jesus had said. He told me this when I was twelve years old. And then all of a sudden . . ."

I asked whether she had lost respect for herself, but she said she hadn't. To the contrary, she never doubted that her principles—and her approach to living a Christian life—reflected God's way, and His will.

Suddenly I was furious with Irene. How could she step into a grieving family and assume that imposing a strict set of religious rules would be good for the children? That she would somehow improve the situation by cracking the whip? She may have been more like her father than she would care to admit.

Between comments, Grandma stared hard at the farm relics she had collected over the years and hung on her kitchen walls. Was she visualizing herself as a child? As a young mother? I believed that as a mother, Irene had probably been unconsciously playing out, perhaps even trying to correct, some of what she had endured as a child under her father's harsh hand. But I wasn't feeling compassion. Not yet.

"I was so sure of what I was doing," Irene repeated. "There

was no question in my mind about my parenting style, but as time went on I began to question my ideas of God. I had lots of struggles. I tried to sort them out, but I also went to my pastors and asked questions about how to live for God."

I wanted to make sure I understood. "You're saying that before you entered the marriage you were sure you were going to affect the family by doing the 'right' thing." When my grandmother nodded, I kept going. "But when you got into it you realized your Christian principles would not be respected by this family, and that led you to question your own ideas about God."

She nodded again.

Later, my grandmother added that she wished she'd had the guts to challenge Ernie, especially when it came to raising the children. She said she should have asked questions and challenged his decisions, but claimed she didn't have the vocabulary. She was so afraid of being cut off verbally that she kept silent to avoid it. Grandma also said that if she had known then what she had learned since, she would not have given up until she and Ernie had talked about their disagreements—and she wouldn't have been afraid.

So who was she really mad at during all those years? Maybe Grandma wasn't only mad about the child-rearing—maybe her anger also reflected a struggle to express herself. She had just described what I myself had experienced—and what Maude had identified as well: a decision to stifle our opinions and silence our voices. I hadn't consciously known that my grandmother and I had that in common, but perhaps at some level I had hoped to connect with her about it and to learn. And now I knew what I needed: encouragement. I wanted Grandma to understand that in spite of my professional success I had trouble speaking up too, especially on my own behalf. Little did I know that Irene Egertson would force me to learn that lesson the hard way.

THERE WERE THREE separate times during the long years I was writing and revising Irene's chapter when my grandmother tried to change the direction of my approach, and, in one instance, to stifle my voice. The first time I was sitting at her kitchen table; she had read a very early version of the chapter—the first chapter I had attempted—and she was unhappy. The book was about HER, she told me; it was HER story, and she didn't think my comments belonged within HER chapter. Why did I mention myself at all? Feeling both surprised and irritated, I reminded her that I was writing for an audience I thought would be interested in my relationships with the subjects, and in what I was learning from them. I reminded her that I, and not she, was the author. After that conversation I kept on writing—at one point even trying to eliminate my voice and do as she asked. But I got so bored with writing a biography that I told myself I didn't care what she thought.

A few years later I heard secondhand that during an event I had not been able to attend, Grandma had announced to my entire family that she didn't like what I had written. I didn't ask for details, and no one offered to provide them. But I do remember someone suggesting that I wait until after Irene died to finish the chapter.

The third incident was the last straw, however. I had reached out to women I thought might be able to suggest subjects for my book, and in the process I had contacted Gloria Steinem. Within a few days her assistant called me back with a message from Gloria that while she really liked the idea, she couldn't provide a subject. She could, however, suggest a good photographer if I needed one. That day I could barely contain my excitement—the undisputed leader of the American Women's Movement had affirmed my idea. I was thrilled and couldn't wait to tell my grandmother the good news. When I finally got her on the phone and relayed the conversation, however, I was struck dumb by her response. After a long pause she said slowly and clearly, victory ringing in her voice, "Well. Now are you finally ready to give your Heavenly Father the credit He deserves for giving you this book?" I have no idea what I said next, or how we ended the conversation. But I took my family's advice and put the book away until after Irene's death. My grandmother and I never discussed her chapter—or my book—again.

BUT BEFORE THAT fateful day, I wanted to consider and write about the other side of Irene's parenting dilemma. No one had ever disputed that when the children had disobeyed or disregarded Irene's rules, Ernie had sided with them instead of his wife.

Beloved among family and friends alike for his fun-loving nature, it was easy to imagine Ernie as a lenient parent who would prefer to avoid conflict. In fact, I couldn't imagine Grandpa getting angry with anyone until the day I saw him give Grandma "the look."

One summer day in my late twenties, I was enjoying dinner with a large group of extended family members. I had just chosen a seat a few places down and across the table from my grandparents when Grandma either said or did something Grandpa didn't like. "Utter contempt" is how I would describe the expression on my grandfather's face as he growled a response that turned his wife's face from rosy pink to ash. I never forgot that moment—the moment I saw Irene's vulnerability and began to feel compassion for what she sometimes experienced as Ernie's wife.

I was glad her marriage had survived; to hear her tell it, this was in large part because of my uncle Joel, who seemed to understand her better than his siblings.

"Well, of course the day I got married was wonderful," Grandma had said. "And also the day we got Joel back, which happened within two weeks of our marriage." Joel had been cared for by Ernie's brother and his wife after Ardis died. "Whether rightly or wrongly, I have felt that having Joel saved my marriage."

This was news to me.

"He didn't talk back to me. He liked me right from the very

beginning and didn't have any trouble adjusting to me that I could see. We got along fine and I was Mama right away." After a pause Grandma said, "Ardis couldn't have him, but as God knew well, 'Irene will take care of him.'" Then she added quickly, "Not that Ardis had any choice, and God did not take her away from the family by any means—God is loving, not cruel. But when things happen you do the best you can and you walk on."

What was Grandma telling herself? Had she unconsciously competed with Ardis? It would be hard not to compare herself to a beautiful and beloved biological parent. Maybe Irene felt she had finally prevailed when Joel came back home and loved her without condition.

"Oh yes . . . Joel loved me, and he didn't have any negative attitude at all. Day to day, he was so happy to see me, and oh my . . . I sensed he was there for a special purpose. But I was also very aware of what Ardis had lost."

I watched my grandmother shake her head slowly back and forth. "To think that she had to lose her life and not have the privilege of raising her own children," she said, characteristically sucking in her breath at the end of her sentences as speakers of Norwegian often do. "I dreamed so often of Ardis. . . so often . . . and of course I had seen her pictures, so in my dreams she looked like the pictures."

I guessed Irene was also at least a little jealous but this wasn't the time to bring it up.

"And so talking to God and talking to Ardis and yet not dealing with her children very well . . . I realized I wasn't doing anything near to what a mother would have done. But I didn't know how," she added, her voice breaking.

And then you had Bruce, I said silently. After three miscarriages, Irene had finally been able to carry a child to term.

"Seven years later, Bruce was born," she said. "And my, what a day that was . . . oh my oh MY oh my oh my," she sighed. "I always thought I would have children, and I was very glad to have the four older ones, but I was also very aware that they were not mine. They were Ernie's and Ardis's children, except for Joel—I felt that he was mine. I had had three miscarriages, and that broke my heart—three different times. I worried that maybe *Three strikes you're out* was a true saying. And I wondered, 'Is that true for me too?'"

"Apparently it wasn't," I said quickly. My sense was that I had heard about this and should have been more careful with my questions. A few friends and family members had been traumatized by miscarriages—I couldn't imagine what it would have been like to have three in a row. I felt sadness and compassion for my grandmother, whose story seemed to evoke intense and often opposing emotions at every turn.

"Well, when I got pregnant the fourth time I changed doctors—I got help, I stayed in bed, and I was taking medication," continued Grandma.

When I expressed surprise she said, "Oh yes—I couldn't even iron . . . there were a lot of things I couldn't do so that when I got cramps I wouldn't deliver the fetus. Even five months along I started getting cramps, so that time I went straight to bed—not for a terribly long time, but long enough so that I kept the baby."

Irene had spent seven long years trying to bring a child to term between the time she got Joel and the day Bruce, her only biological child, was born. That was the day Irene felt like she truly belonged to the Egertson family.

ANOTHER STRESS POINT within my grandparents' marriage was the number of times Ernie moved his family—at least fifteen times, according to Irene, who said they had probably lived in more than twenty different homes. I also knew that had powerfully affected my father, who eventually made a list of all the houses he had lived in with his parents. But that was never the focus of my conversations with Irene. Although Grandma didn't agree with all the moves, she accepted her husband's decisions and tried to make the best of them for the sake of her family.

"What happened in California?" I asked about their move west, remembering how much I loved walking to the house she lived in just down the street from ours. Fifty-five years later, when I walked past that house again, the night-blooming jasmine still climbed up the arbor near the front door.

"My sons always thought I was too nervous to drive, but once we moved to the California suburbs, I had no way to get away from the house," recalled Grandma, "so I signed up for driving class." Although it took her an additional few years and another move, Irene eventually passed the test and earned her driver's license. She also found the time and confidence to pursue two other passions: Bible study and painting.

"I had put off getting my license in California to attend a new Bible study class that was only offered in a few cities across the country," explained my grandmother. "When Ernie told me we were moving to Tulsa, I was devastated to give that up. But when we got there, I found out that a church near our house was going to offer the same series of classes, and I knew God had taken care of me once again."

I was eight years old when my grandparents moved into an attractive brick rambler located a mile from our own lovely home in Tulsa. Back in 1962, I loved going to their house for a Scandinavian version of goulash and the chance to play outside with their nervous rat terrier, Oscar. During those days, my grandmother wore her blonde hair swept up in the graceful French roll so popular at the time. Even at home she dressed in clothing and jewelry perfectly suited to her face and body.

Irene was never more beautiful than the day she stood before her family at her twenty-fifth wedding anniversary party, held at our new house in St. Louis. I had just turned ten; I remember admiring my grandma, who seemed happy and energetic. And why wouldn't she be? During those years, as her husband thrived at work, she was raising a healthy teenager, living in a house she loved, and attending a church that stimulated her both spiritually and socially. Grandma had also found a painting class, which introduced a period of prolific creativity into her life.

"My sixth grade teacher was the only person who told me I could draw," said Irene, recalling her dream to be an artist. "At one point I had the opportunity to take art lessons from a neighbor, but my father said it would interfere with my confirmation studies," she added. "Later, as I was raising children, there wasn't time for art because I spent all my extra time at church. So I found other ways to express myself. I dressed my body as though I were painting a picture. I made special meals for my family and turned every holiday event into a party. Her children still remember the beautiful candle holders Irene carved out of Ivory soap and placed on wall mouldings around her dining room and beyond—an ingenious but labor-intensive way to illuminate the memorable wedding reception she put on single-handedly for her sister. "I also decorated my dining room table for each occasion with things I had on hand, and often with items other people didn't want, by putting them together in attractive ways," said Irene.

ONE MORNING I drove my grandmother back from two hours of shopping for things other people didn't want and found myself thinking about her quirkiness. Her artistic nature was innate; she had adopted her father's unrelenting version of Christianity; she idolized her courageous mother and revered the pastors who had guided her in her youth and beyond. She believed wholeheartedly in the institution of marriage and firmly believed a woman's place was in the home. Yet she was proud of the women in her family, like me, who had chosen other options. Suddenly I wondered who her female role models would have been.

Obviously, Irene had learned how to be a wife and mother by watching her own mother and grandmother—both strong, highly principled women. Mrs. Sivertson, the respected neighbor who had helped her family escape her father, made an impression, too. And then I remembered one of Irene's sisters, whom I had met but never gotten to know—the one who had become a pilot.

"How did Ruth achieve that dream?" I asked my grandmother one day. "Things like economics and families that don't support your vision can destroy your dreams unless you have the guts it takes to pursue them," she answered. "My sister had that kind of guts."

In the 1930s, Ruth Egeberg became a pilot despite an utter lack of support from her immediate family. Fortunately, Ruth's uncle stepped in and successfully challenged the male instructors who initially wouldn't allow Ruth to participate. "This was after Amelia Earhart but long before women were generally recognized as being intelligent or responsible enough to fly and care for a plane," remembered Irene. "The write-ups about Ruth getting her pilot's license were big articles—because no women did that then."

Irene's oldest sister exhibited a different kind of strength when she eschewed marriage to support herself by working in an office downtown during an era when women were expected to marry and raise children. Well-known as a tireless and outspoken worker within her church and, eventually, within her retirement community, Berthina's enthusiasm and interest in everyone she met made a lasting impression on others until the day she died in her late nineties. Apparently, my grandmother was in good company within this family of determined, opinionated women.

Come to think of it, maybe I was, too. I had often felt sorry for myself for not having role models within my family who worked outside the home—or supported their families, as my sister and I later did. Several of my aunts had professions, but all had opted to stay at home and raise their children. When it was time for me to have children I knew I wouldn't be a good stay-at-home mom, but could never forgive my husband for being available to do just that. Garbled as the messages within the feminist movement often were back then, wasn't the point of it all to give women a choice? And a voice?

Perhaps I hadn't been looking in the right places. While I was seeking women who had won the battle, maybe most of them had still been fighting it. Meanwhile—had I known about them—some of the strongest role models were closer than I thought: Anna Egeberg, who chose emotional and physical safety for herself and her family over financial security. Ruth Egeberg, who broke countless gender rules to fly a plane; her sister, Berthina, who chose to support herself and her mother rather than pursue marriage. And finally, my own grandmother, who clung to her faith—often by her fingernails—despite resistance and criticism from her own family.

AFTER YEARS OF moving around and finally feeling settled, Irene and Ernie would move one final time. When Grandpa retired in 1971, he and my grandmother moved across the country from Oklahoma back to Minnesota. For the next six years they lived in a tiny double bungalow located across from an airport runway. In spite of the noise, Irene established her home—and her kitchen table—as a place for her family to gather. In particular, she loved visiting with her grown grandchildren.

"One at a time they would come to my house and we would talk for hours," said Grandma, smiling. "And oh my, we could even discuss controversial subjects without getting angry." For Irene, these conversations presented a chance to be understood and accepted by a new generation of adults within her growing family. "Why, they saw me as a person with ideas worth listening to," she recalled.

I remembered those days too, as I was one of her most frequent visitors from 1973 to 1976. Often on Saturday mornings my older brother and I would drive the short distance from Augsburg College to Lake Nokomis in his putty-colored VW Beetle to have coffee with Grandma and Grandpa. Grandma was at her best in her kitchen, where she and Grandpa would listen to our problems for hours on end. Of course, she challenged our ideas, especially those having anything to do with Christianity or religion in general. But most of the time she was respectful—during those visits she became a version of herself that we all loved being around. Perhaps it was because she didn't feel threatened; Grandma had always claimed she did better with teenagers than small children. That happy dynamic played out for a period of at least ten years, as Irene's grandchildren attended college in or near Minneapolis.

Eventually, my grandparents moved to a small home in an older Minneapolis suburb, where they lived together for the last few years of Ernie's life. After he died, Grandma told me she had depended on many of the skills she learned in her twenties to provide full-time caregiving for Grandpa, who suffered from dementia until he died in 1995. For the next eleven years, Irene lived alone in that house, where she enjoyed dividing her time among visiting with family and friends, attending church functions, decorating each room, and producing her art.

One day near the end of our interviews I followed the sweep of my grandmother's arm as she pointed out specific items hanging on the crowded walls of her tiny kitchen. It was hard to focus on any one thing, as every inch of wall space was covered with miniature paintings, tiny framed mirrors, family photos, and antique tools. Irene had also turned her adjoining dining and living rooms into a visual tribute—a museum of sorts, devoted to her past. Scattered among the chairs and lamps were several small tables, each set with a themed display. One featured antique dolls and doll heads—an area I found to be a little creepy. Another held multiple framed photos, and the coffee table in front of the velveteen couch was adorned with clear glass angels, trees, and reindeer.

Also scattered around the room were antique candle holders and colorful pillows, many covered with patchworks of Ernie's old ties. Irene had carefully arranged children's toys in one corner, while in another, a year-round Christmas tree featured the colored ornaments she loved so well.

A few yards away, the dining room table remained buried under Irene's projects: photos of Ernie she was arranging into a collage; remnants from the decorated box she'd made for a recently-confirmed great-grandson; the Christmas cards she reused and sent to friends and family. If I hadn't known this woman, I would have worried about her tendencies to hoard. I imagined the clutter might also have triggered a major reaction for anyone with claustrophobia. But these rooms—and those years—served an important purpose for my grandmother.

"This is what I do instead of thinking about the bad things that happened in my life," explained Grandma when I asked about her compulsion to decorate. "It helps me remember the many good things."

That's when I understood for the first time that Irene's cluttered walls were her way of retelling and reclaiming the story of her life. It was a way she could fully express herself—without comment or complaint from others—in a language she loved. Those rooms had become her palette—a place where Irene had become the artist she always wanted to be. A safe place where my grandmother could finally heal.

~

In 2009, at the age of ninety-four, Irene died quietly at the home of her youngest son, Bruce, and his wife, Mary, who lived in suburban Minneapolis. Earlier that week I had felt a sudden sense of acute anxiety and grief associated with my grandmother, so I called my uncle and asked to visit Grandma for what I knew would be the last time. When I walked into the living room, she was lying in a hospital bed on her side with her eyes closed. Sitting beside the bed, I told her I loved her, and while she acknowledged my presence, she also made it clear she didn't want to be touched. Later I learned that she had been receiving light doses of morphine for pain, probably the result of her impossibly frail and thin condition at the end.

"Mom died sometime between 5:00 and 5:30 p.m.," said Bruce when I asked for details about her actual death. "I was not with her at her final breath but had said goodbye. As I was about to leave for my evening job, Mary checked on her and told me to come back in, as she thought Mom had just passed." I couldn't think of a sweeter or more appropriate way for Grandma to leave.

A few days after that I delivered a eulogy at my grandmother's large and lengthy funeral—something she had asked me to do years earlier. I figured all of the people Grandma had chosen to speak were, like me, executing some very clear and specific instructions, especially the fourth and final speaker. From the lectern of the large Lutheran church Irene had attended for many years, Bruce read the scriptures and delivered the messages his mother had preached throughout her life to anyone who would listen. This time, however, he delivered them to a captive audience.

Because this time, finally, my grandmother's voice would be heard without argument or interruption. By planning her own service, Grandma had ensured it would be a celebration of her Christian faith and a tribute to the beloved Savior she had served all her life. On that day, my grandmother's clan not only heard the words she herself had written, but followed her step-by-step instructions to the letter.

That day, Irene Egertson had the last word.

IT WAS THE last day of August 2017 and I was feeling unusually melancholy. Twenty-four hours after bringing home a new puppy to help soothe the pain of losing my fourth greyhound, the animal I referred to as "the dog of my life," I was feeling worse than ever. How could I be this sad when the sky was so blue, the temperature so perfect, my life so calm? That day I felt a little crazy—a word I used carefully lately, as more of my friends and family members addressed and talked openly about mental illness: depression, anxiety, bipolar disorder, anorexia, OCD. Suddenly I felt even sadder; I knew Grandma had been treated for depression. She may have experienced Post Traumatic Stress Disorder (PTSD), too, as a result of what she witnessed and experienced as a child. Is that what Grandma had? Did she die a decade too soon—before we were able to pinpoint, understand, and forgive her for behaviors that may have been out of her control?

Now that I had become educated about brain disease and the way each one manifests differently, I was prepared for the attending behaviors of other people I loved. Had I ever given Grandma that latitude?

I remember one night in particular when my grandmother had a meltdown right in her own living room, in front of her husband, grown children, and other members of her extended family. Typically, when one of her children came to town for a visit, Grandma would host a dinner and invite any local family members who could attend. That night, as they sat around her dining room table after dinner, Grandma suddenly just seemed to break down—with angry tears and accusations—in a way that scared everyone but my husband, a licensed social worker who eventually talked Grandma into going to the ER.

For many years there were hurt feelings about what my grandmother had said that night. But as I learned more about mental illness I began to see Irene differently; had I understood more about what Grandma was experiencing, I might have had more compassion and forgiven her sooner for some of the things she had said and done over the years. Had my grandmother suffered from an undiagnosed mental illness? Was I too hard on her?

Obviously, I will never know.

IRENE HAD BEEN married to Ernie for fifty-seven years by the time he died. Throughout her marriage, she grappled with demons—internal conflicts between her need for independence and her fear of loss, between her desire to be outspoken and her fear of being shut down. Time and again Irene believed she had to choose between pleasing her spouse and obeying her God. Yet she never stopped believing that a woman should please her husband to maintain a happy marriage.

"After all you've been through, I'm not sure I understand why you would think that," I said one day during an early-morning interview.

"Well, to have a really good marriage, it has to go both ways," she explained. "I think women today are still the pleasers more than men. In my experience, which is quite limited, men still seem to have more control. And that's not bad, if the man is wise enough to also be a pleaser. Because until you've learned to please your spouse, you don't have real love."

As a young wife, my grandmother came to believe that pleasing Grandpa would require giving up the devout Christian lifestyle she had known and loved as a child. Unfortunately, as her children grew up she moved even further away from the lifestyle her faith dictated. And though she never specified how, I think she experienced guilt over the lively evenings she and my grandfather spent with their best friends after the children were grown, good times that included formerly forbidden cocktails. I would guess she wasn't allowed to dance, either, as she was growing up—a rule that must have created at least a little consternation on one night in particular, when, in her eighties, Irene enjoyed some serious fun dancing at a family wedding. But I believe she blamed herself most for not speaking up when her children broke the rules by swearing, drinking, staying out late, or arguing with her—a clear sign of disrespect in the Christian world she preferred.

I thought again about why so many women choose to squash their opinions and subvert their values. We must believe, at some level, that the price of speaking up is too high. Under patriarchy, women learn to be careful not only about when and if they speak up, but also how they do it. Will we lose our jobs? Our families? Our homes? The lucky ones among us eventually come to realize that the cost of NOT speaking up can be even higher. And I think Irene would agree with me on that.

When I asked what advice she'd like to give other women based on what she'd learned, Irene was very clear. "Don't give up your values," she said, shaking her head firmly. "In my day, girls lived according to the values of their fathers first, and then of their husbands, once they were married. I believe I was so insecure and so much in love that I wanted to please Ernie above everything. I also believed 'above everything' meant giving up my faith in God. So I put my husband above my faith and I saved my marriage—but I was living a double standard."

"Women should be honest with their thoughts and opinions and learn to talk about them," added my grandmother. "When I was young, it was not a girl's place to reveal her own ideas. Even grown women did not have permission to speak up and give opinions. It wasn't until the early 1970s that I felt I had the right to be heard."

I couldn't remember a time when my grandmother didn't express her opinions. She must have done so in spite of the conflict she felt. Or maybe the rules were different outside of the marriage.

When I asked my uncles for examples of how their mother spoke her mind, I learned that in the early 1960s, when my Uncle Joel brought his young and beautiful fiancée to meet his mother, Irene had looked at him in all seriousness and said, "You told me to treat her like all the other girls you were going to marry."

Many years later, at his mother's fiftieth wedding anniversary celebration, Joel recited a beautiful line from *Les Misérables*. He meant to honor Irene by showing publicly that he respected and understood her devotion to God. Expecting his mother to be moved when he quoted, "To love another person is to see the face of God," he was surprised to learn she was anything but appreciative.

"After the event," he recalled, "Mom told me she wished I hadn't used that quote because it wasn't biblical and defied God's commandment to love God above all." I knew exactly how my uncle felt, remembering similar times when my attempts to please Irene had fallen flat.

But Grandma was dead serious as she continued with her recollections. "I never agreed entirely with Gloria Steinem and the women's movement. Not all women wanted to be liberated from men and that caused a division among women," she said. "But I did want to be heard and I didn't have permission until I saw my daughters-in-law speaking out about their opinions. Only then did I finally believe I had the right—and the courage—to express myself."

At that point I could have shared my observations about how she often spoke out, whether or not she felt she had the right. Instead, I asked what she thought the cost of suppressing her thoughts had been.

"Personally, I felt stifled. For my family, the price was a lack of openness—and without openness, a family cannot be truly safe or loving." That day—during our last interview—Irene sat back and paused before adding, "Here's what I would say to women of any age: Don't take yourself so seriously—be reckless. Women still seem to be too concerned about how they look and how they behave. I think women should do what they want in spite of what people will say. So what if you make a mistake? After two days or two weeks, the things you do and say will be forgotten by most people anyway, so why not do today what you won't be able to do tomorrow?"

I wanted to pursue this line, but Irene wasn't finished. "When I turned eighty, something happened to me," she confessed. "All of a sudden, I lost the self-consciousness I had lived with all my life. I lost the feeling that I didn't have the right to be heard. I let go of my concern over what others might think, and I felt free. I was no longer inhibited about saying what I thought and felt, and I expressed it—to my family, my friends, and even my pastor."

That transition didn't go unnoticed, I thought, as I watched my grandmother glow with pride. Feeling muzzled truly was a lifelong struggle for this woman. And she was right about the change in her behaviors: as Grandma aged, I watched her move from fear and uncertainty about her life and decisions to confidence and independence. For example, when she finally left the home she had shared with Grandpa to live near several of her sisters in a large senior complex, her children realized she'd been planning the transition for a long time—perhaps years—without anyone knowing about it. While the rest of us had been wringing our hands over where Irene would spend her old age, she had been carefully and independently planning for her future.

During the last few years of her life, even as she grew more frail, I'd visit my grandmother in her apartment—filled with the familiar items she still loved—and we'd resume our ongoing conversation. We continued to laugh together at the silly parts of life and argued about whether my faith was any of her business. I knew she was still intensely interested in what every single member of her family was up to, so I depended on her for news about my relatives. I also knew she was one of the few people who truly understood my artistic daughter. No doubt Irene saw some of herself in her great-granddaughter's personality and sensibilities.

At age ninety-four, Irene Egertson loved her Lord, her family, her friends, her life, and her memories. Best of all, she still loved me.

COMMUNITY TREASURE

Sadie Anton

One wintry evening in the early 1940s, two women approached a set of steep steps located near the edge of downtown Minneapolis. These steps led straight up to the bridge connecting Nicollet Island to the neighborhood where the Lebanese community lived and worked. Normally, a walk over the Mississippi River would take no more than twenty minutes. But tonight, the two women would have to push the heavy box of frozen chickens up the steps, across the bridge, and down several city streets . . . in the dark.

But the two friends continued their trek with determination, laughing at themselves as they reached the streetcar line. They knew the "motor man" would help them stow their box during the ride and lift it off again when they reached their stop. Then it would be another short walk to the church, where they would drop off the box in preparation for the following weekend. After months of planning, the women of St. Maron Maronite Catholic Church would cook and serve the chickens to dozens of happy patrons at the annual fundraising dinner.

Sixty years later, at age ninety-six, one of them would still be cooking chickens for the St. Maron's fundraiser. That woman was Sadie Anton, matriarch of the Northeast Minneapolis Lebanese community.

I met Sadie through her friend Tony, one of the happiest, most optimistic people I've ever known. Born in Lebanon, Tony had moved to the United States in the 1980s, after falling in love with a beautiful, strawberry-blonde American whom he met in France. In 1999, Tony moved his wife and their four children from South Minneapolis to Northeast, where he would be closer to the Lebanese community. That's when he got to know Sadie.

Four years later, I met Tony at a neighborhood barbecue. By that time I had started on two chapters and was looking for more diversity among my next subjects. That evening Tony was so engaging—and so proud of his culture—that I wanted to know more. After dinner, when I told him about my book and asked whether he knew anyone within the Lebanese community who might be an appropriate subject, Tony took a long puff on his cigar and then broke into an enormous, toothy smile. "I have the perfect person for you—everyone knows Sadie Anton because she's been around forever. We call her Aunt Sadie; I will introduce you!" he promised. A few weeks later I had a date to meet Tony and Sadie after church.

I'D BETTER LOOK *good today,* I thought as I chose a plaid, wool jacket and black pants to wear to St. Maron's. Tony had told me the women of the congregation dressed up for Sunday service, and I wanted to fit in. I knew where the church was; I'd driven over the bridge to Sadie's neighborhood many times on my way to Emily's Lebanese Deli, one of my favorite spots for lunch. More than once, I had noticed the butterscotch-colored building located on the left side of the road a couple of blocks before Emily's. I also remember being initially surprised that it was a church. It didn't look at all like the red brick or gray stone Lutheran churches that so heavily populate the Twin Cities. It did, however, share a particular kind of beauty that places of worship around the world seem to have in common.

That day the large church lot was full, and spaces on the side streets were taken as well, so I had to park on the busy street in front. I wandered around the building until I found a large side door that led to the sanctuary. Out of the corner of my eye I thought I recognized Tony's wife, Gaelle, but decided I didn't have enough time to approach her; I was in a hurry to find a seat where I could get a glimpse of Sadie. Typically, I would sit in the back of a church I hadn't previously attended to avoid participating in activities I might not understand. But I knew Sadie would be in the choir standing next to Tony, so I bravely chose a seat halfway up the aisle. Then I looked around.

I noticed the women first. Tony wasn't kidding when he said they dressed up. My attire was almost manly compared to the elegant dresses, jewelry, and makeup so tastefully on display around me. But it was the abundance of glossy, dark brown hair that caught and held my attention. Wherever I looked at eye level, I saw thick, gorgeous waves of healthy-looking hair. And it didn't belong to just the women; with the exception of a few people, including myself, it was shared by just about everyone who wasn't gray.

Reminding myself not to stare, I turned my attention to the choir. Tony was hard to miss, towering above most of the other choir members. When I noticed the very top of a white head standing to Tony's left, I realized I wouldn't get a good look at Sadie until later. I had hoped to learn something about this woman by observing her from a distance; after all, Tony had offered to share with me a relationship he cared about deeply, and I wanted to make a good impression. I was about to ask a beloved representative of his community to share her opinions, stories, and advice with someone Tony himself barely knew. This meeting was my first attempt to engage a woman who seemed like the perfect subject, and to earn Sadie's trust I would need to be both charming and respectful from the moment I met her. So I spent the rest of the morning looking for cultural cues by listening carefully to the service—conducted in Arabic except for a few announcements—and the choir, which sang in unison without accompaniment. As I settled into the knowledge that for the next hour or so I wouldn't understand a thing, I tried to imagine what it would be like to hear those exact words every week for more than ninety years.

When the service ended, I stood up and looked toward where I'd seen Sadie. She was gone, so I figured I'd meet her by the door as we had planned. As I waited, I smiled at the children, greeted a woman I had recognized from an earlier life, spoke with Tony, and looked for the white head I had seen in the choir. Twenty minutes later, when Tony realized I hadn't found her, he went looking for Sadie himself. Within a few minutes, he was back. I watched a short, dignified woman in a beautiful plaid suit walk slowly toward me. I wondered whether I was in trouble.

"Jen-ney?" she inquired, looking up into my face as she enunciated each syllable.

"I'm so sorry . . ." I began.

Clearly impatient to get this over with, Sadie politely suggested we find a quiet place in the church to chat. But Tony had other ideas.

"Let's go out for coffee," he said, flashing a smile that no one—not even Sadie—could resist.

"Oh, I thought we'd just stay here," she said, attempting to be firm.

"Oh no," said Tony. "I have my car all ready. Let's go to Jacob's."

And that was that.

~

IF YOU LIVE in Minneapolis city proper, chances are you've been to the neighborhood the locals call "Nordeast." Northeast Minneapolis actually includes thirteen neighborhoods and has been home to a host of ethnic groups for over a century.

Driving east from busy downtown Minneapolis, you take Hennepin Avenue over the Mississippi River. On the other side is a popular, well-preserved area that draws a steady stream of visitors with its eclectic variety of bars and restaurants, hair salons, coffee shops, specialty stores, and fabulous high-rise condos overlooking the river. As you drive north on University Avenue, you cross a small bridge that drops you off in a blue-collar neighborhood of modest homes and apartment buildings. Two blocks down University on the right is the house where Sadie lived for over sixty years. Four blocks further on the left is St. Maron's. On that short route, you will have seen approximately half of the twenty-block Lebanese community and followed the path that defined Sadie Anton's world for over a hundred years.

Jacob's 101 closed in the spring of 2005, but that afternoon in 2003 it was business as usual. As we entered the bar at the back of the restaurant, Tony was the undisputed center of attention, keeping up a steady banter with each person we passed.

Sadie and I kept walking. I never found out whether she approved of the bawdy conversation Tony was having with the bartender, because as soon as we walked through the doorway leading into the restaurant, Sadie got busy.

She greeted patrons seated at every single table we passed—and Jacob's had plenty of tables. There were lots of smiles and a few stares at me. Men, women, children, teenagers—everyone there, it seemed—said hello to Sadie. By the time we reached our table, I realized that most of the people seated within this restaurant were members of Sadie's neighborhood "family."

That day, as Tony helped me and Sadie get used to each other, I found out just how much he admired his friend.

"Sadie relates to all the different generations and all the different families," he said. "She's involved with everything at St. Maron's, and people call her Aunt Sadie. She's had the name for the last twenty-five years."

Sadie nodded.

"And she's very eloquent," he continued. "She delivers a speech at every special occasion."

Up until that moment I had felt I needed to show deference by watching and listening. Sadie had moved slowly but quite regally through the crowd. At the table, she spoke slowly and distinctly, in phonetically perfect English, each time Tony asked her a question. I had been as polite and attentive as I knew how to be, but now, if I intended to establish my own relationship with Sadie, I had to step in.

"It sounds like you're a good speaker, Sadie."

"Well, I try my best, Jenney."

Encouraged that she had called me by name, I kept going with a comment on how she seemed to know everyone in the room. She smiled and told me that yes, she knew everyone because she had lived in the same community all her life. By that time we had ordered lunch, but Sadie said her stomach wasn't feeling all that great, so I decided not to waste any more time. "What kind of special occasions was Tony referring to—what do you speak about?"

When she raised her eyebrows and smiled, I breathed a sigh of relief. I sat back in my chair as Sadie listed the types of church events she was called upon to promote—she became especially animated when Tony mentioned the annual dinner. Finally the ice had broken; Sadie was enjoying herself.

A few minutes later Sadie began talking about her life and Tony heard a few details even he hadn't known.

"I was the youngest of seven children—four girls and three boys," she began. "Our parents spoke Arabic, which has many forms. We lost one brother, Peter, at age twenty-two. He had kidney problems that required surgery, but people didn't believe in surgery at that time so they wouldn't let the doctors operate."

Sadie proceeded with a highly condensed chronological account of her life, beginning with whom she had lost: her brother Martin, who met with an auto accident at age forty-five. I couldn't imagine myself in her place; the thought of losing my sister or either of my brothers was unbearable. Sadie's sister in Missouri had been ninety-four when she died, but her brother Si was still around. She didn't mention the two other sisters, so I never knew what happened to them. I knew from Tony that Sadie had strong, loving relationships within her family and beyond, but that wasn't apparent as she rattled off a few more facts.

She had lost her father during the summer before ninth grade, so her mother was left with the children, who all worked to help support the family. Sadie worked part-time and completed high school but didn't have the funds to attend college. I was getting the impression that this was a woman who navigated life by simply putting one foot in front of the other, no matter what went on around her.

"I did go to beauty school at night," she explained, "but that career didn't materialize because I got a part-time job in an office doing counter work. I was sixteen or seventeen, and I wanted to better myself but continued in the office job instead, to learn switchboard, bookkeeping, and other skills. I stayed with that company for seventeen years."

For some reason, I had always thought that during Sadie's time most women worked at home exclusively. Now I was beginning to realize that while many women *did* work outside the home, it was typically the men who talked about work—*their* work, of course.

Next, Sadie told me about her marriage. In 1934, at the age of twenty-five, she married Anthony D. Anton, a man from her parish whom she had known all her life. Their first home was located less than a mile from St. Maron's, and in 1938 they moved a few blocks south to a house Sadie still occupied—by the time we met, she had lived there for sixty-six years.

I remained quiet as Sadie continued to talk; to this day I'm not sure why I didn't ask specific questions about her extended family. I know very little about them and that's the way I think Sadie wanted it. She did share the basics about her immediate family: that her husband did the plumbing, painting, and electrical work; that he worked for Honeywell; and that he passed away in 1974, which meant they lived together for forty years. After Anthony died she lived with their son, Robert—her only child—until he got married. Sadie told me he was well educated, had worked as an accountant for American Express Financial, and died at the age of fifty-seven. That was all she said.

As Sadie talked, I thought about other ninety-four-year-olds I had known—most had probably experienced a fair amount of loss by that age, and Sadie had, too. I also noticed that no one at the table was asking Sadie for more detail about her son or husband—both Tony and I let that go. Only later did I realize why.

People expect to lose their parents, although most don't have to deal with it at age thirteen. Most of us don't expect our siblings to die all at once, either; Sadie had lost five of hers, but that seemed typical. Most women who are married to men also understand that if they live to age seventy-five, they'll probably survive their husbands. But we all hope to die before our children—and from what I've observed, losing a child at any age brings unspeakable sorrow. So when Sadie stopped talking about her family, I didn't push and neither did Tony.

"When I was a girl, life revolved around the church," Sadie began, when I asked about her childhood. "Children were drilled and taught church. My parents were very religious and we went to church every Sunday. As children, we couldn't miss Mass, either, even if we were sick. If we were able to be up and around, we had no excuse. Besides, the church was two blocks away from our house."

"So there was no escaping church," I confirmed.

"No, there was no escape. But we didn't want to escape," said Sadie. "It was the center of our lives. Once a month our parents would hold a dinner in the church. Each family would prepare an assigned dish at home and bring it for the meal on Sunday. On Saturday, the young people would scrub and prepare the church hall for the meal. We enjoyed doing that."

After a brief silence, she continued. "No, I've always liked being involved. God wanted me here and gave me the life and happiness I had with my husband and family. No one can erase that; I had a good life."

Had? I treaded carefully. "What was so good about your life?"

"I had a good marriage," she replied. "My husband and I always had the same likes and dislikes. If we had a misunderstanding, we sat and talked about it. We never had any ill feeling; we just erased that by talking things over, and then we were back to where we started, on friendly terms."

Sadie was the third women of three who had emphasized communication as being the key to good relationships. Before continuing, Sadie sat for a moment and thought about what she'd just said. "It's true—we agreed on everything, and our parents didn't interfere."

Then she added, "Once you're married, that's your bed, and you lie in it. Maybe the mother will give you a lecture if she knows you're wrong, and in our day you listened to your folks; you respected them even after you were married. You took their opinion on many things."

I thought about my two unsuccessful marriages and wondered how it would be possible to agree on everything with anyone.

"How do you think that compares to today?" I asked.

"It's not the same," answered Sadie. "I think today people are different; the generations have changed. The young people today don't observe their religion. In our day, religion always came first," she said, shrugging her shoulders.

Sadie and my grandmother had both enjoyed lives that revolved around church. But talking to Sadie about her faith was much different than having a similar conversation with Irene. Maybe it was because the Maronite Catholic Church was so different from what I grew up with as a Lutheran. And Sadie wasn't trying to save me, either; she never asked about my personal beliefs or referred to her own. So I was engaged in a way that surprised me—almost like I wanted Sadie to talk me into getting involved with a church. In 2004, at age fifty, I still mostly rejected the notion that Christianity had much to offer me personally; but Sadie hadn't mentioned God or Jesus. She simply talked about the community she had loved all her life.

So I asked Sadie what she thought had happened to religion. I wasn't surprised to hear that she thought children watched too much TV—other people her age had similar complaints. But I wondered what that had to do with religion. And how it might relate back to marriage.

"Well, we didn't have radio and television to distract children from school and church—the two most important ways they learn," explained Sadie. In her day, the church community kept children close to their parents beyond Sunday service and taught values that would be important to making a marriage work. It was also the way couples got to know each other—but that was rapidly becoming a thing of the past. So was the notion that parents should have a say about whom their children chose to marry.

That led to Sadie's advice about marriage. I hadn't told her yet that my first marriage had failed and my second wasn't working all that well either. Frankly, I was in need of advice from someone whose marriage had succeeded. I wanted to hear from a woman who managed her marriage differently from the way I was mismanaging mine.

"When you marry," said Sadie, "you should make up your mind you're going to stay with the person all your life. So you should marry of your own people because you have similar likes and dislikes. You speak the same language; you understand each other. And you know you'll agree on how you'll raise the children—which religion they'll be. Your spouse will never be able to throw religion at you because you're of the same faith and you have the same beliefs."

Well, I had sort of tried that twice. The first time, I married a man who had grown up in a conservative Lutheran congregation; in fact, I had walked away in a huff from a very brief meeting with his pastor, who refused to officiate with mine because our brand of Lutherans ordained women. "You just said that to the wrong woman," I had hissed under my breath as we left his office. The next time, I married a man who had actually made it through the Lutheran Seminary but opted not to be ordained. So I'd married within my faith twice. But I hadn't grown up attending church regularly with either of my husbands, nor did we attend together after we were married—and that seemed to be Sadie's message.

Our conversation reminded me of the Jewish community I had grown up with in St. Louis—even then it was the culture and the way my friends talked about being Jewish that appealed to me. Not that I wasn't proud to be Lutheran; for me, the Jewish community felt like a second wide and strong safety net . . . a place where I was always welcome.

Maybe that's why Sadie's description of a bygone era—a time when her community clearly understood and agreed on specific ways of making major life decisions—felt surprisingly comforting to me. It sounded safe.

ON THE MORNING of our second interview, Sadie and I had gone again to Jacob's 101 Bar. We'd had a long, enlightening conversation, and I had begun to understand exactly why this woman was so loved by her community. But there was one topic she would not discuss. In fact, she told me point-blank that she would not comment on politics or the current war with Iraq.

I had spoken about war with some of the other women I had by this time begun to interview, and while most didn't elaborate on their feelings, I thought I knew where they stood on war in general, if not this particular conflict. But Sadie would have no talk of it at all. This made sense; I was interviewing a woman who had grown up speaking Arabic, and 9/11 was only two years behind us. Had she experienced discrimination because she was Lebanese? I knew others who were being detained at the airport because they *looked* Middle Eastern. Was she worried that she would get lumped in with terrorists? I would never have a chance to ask.

I did know that in the early 1900s, Sadie's father had traveled to the US, leaving his wife and four of their children—two girls and two boys—in Lebanon. He'd heard that America was a "rich" country where it wouldn't take long to earn lots of money and make a nice life. His plan was to work for one year in the US and then go back to Lebanon. When he arrived in America along with relatives who had the same idea, he encountered a strange country, harsh weather, and a language barrier he hadn't anticipated. He sent for his family anyway, and a few years later, on February 28, 1909, Sadie was born in a little house on the corner of Main Street and First Avenue Northeast in Minneapolis.

Sadie recalled that when she was six years old, a lady from the parish took her to Everett School, where she started kindergarten. Most of the children were Lebanese, but at that time Lebanon was controlled by Syria, so they were known as the Syrian people.

"My husband was born in Lebanon, and he came here when he was four or five years old. He adapted well here."

"Did your family speak Arabic at home?" I had asked.

"Yes, until I went to school. And my husband and I spoke Arabic in our home, too. My son could speak Arabic but couldn't read and write it."

That was over fifty years ago; could it be possible that Sadie was afraid her name, her past, and her language could actually hurt her now?

I got my answer when Sadie reviewed and corrected what I had written. In shaky but beautifully formed cursive, every word perfectly lined up with the next, she had written the following note: "I was born in America, my native country, and I'm a true American."

Her final comment on the subject was this: "Our people went to night school to learn the English language. They were true Americans."

AT THE END of February 2005, more than a year after I'd spoken with Sadie, I realized with alarm that I didn't even know whether she was still alive. After all, she'd be ninety-six.

Since I'd last met with Sadie, I'd been working on the book sporadically. I had also recently discovered that in the transfer of documents among disks and between computers, I'd lost all the copy I'd written and all the transcribed notes from my interviews with Sadie. Our taped conversations were still intact, but they would need to be transcribed for a second time.

Then I remembered that St. Maron's publicized its events on the sign in front of the church. *I need to attend an event,* I thought, feeling guilty about the lapse in my communication with Sadie. I had made a commitment to write and finish a chapter about her. She had graciously helped me with that and I needed to let her know, in person, that I was still working on her story.

A few weeks later, I found myself at Emily's, treating my daughter to lunch. We were right down the street from where Sadie lived and I decided to ask the waitress about her.

"I have a question I'm wondering if you could answer," I said to the cheerful, dark-haired woman who had worked at the restaurant for as long as I could remember. For most of our meal she'd been sitting in the corner peeling a huge mound of garlic cloves; now, she was walking across the small floor. And her smile indicated her willingness to listen.

"I have a friend. She's quite elderly, with beautiful white hair, and she's very involved with St. Maron's. Her name is Sadie and I'm wondering if you know her."

"Oh, you must mean Sadie Anton!" replied the woman. "She was in here a couple of weeks ago. Yeah, she's still around. I think she just turned ninety-six . . . but her brother died a few months ago. He was in his nineties, too."

So she was still alive. But her last remaining brother was gone—which meant that in terms of her immediate family, she was now more alone than ever.

According to the waitress, Sadie had been coming to Emily's for years. I thought about the church, Jacob's 101, and Emily's, each a differently colored thread within the fabric of the Lebanese community—with Sadie as one of its master weavers. With that image in mind I renewed my resolve to see my friend at least one more time.

IT WAS EARLY April 2005, and the day couldn't have been more perfect. As I gazed out the window of the lakeside cottage I'd rented for the off-season, I felt satisfied with what I'd written after transcribing—for the second time—my first interview with Sadie. But I still had to tackle the other side of the tape: a slow, tedious process I could only tolerate in half-hour intervals.

As I listened, I recalled the day of the recorded conversation. Similar to others I'd interviewed for the book, Sadie was one of those women whose words didn't always come easily. The pauses between comments were sometimes a minute or more. Impatient as I felt, however, I believed the nuggets I'd uncover by transcribing the tape would be worth the excavation.

During that second interview, when I asked Sadie broadly about how she felt society had changed, she took her time answering. "Today, society is very open," she began. "In the early days, we didn't use the way we dressed to express our thoughts and feelings. We had more respect for ourselves." After a long pause, she continued. "The woman stayed at home and raised her family. And she made sure her children were educated and showed respect—in the way they dressed and how they associated with other people."

By this time, I was pretty sure we were about to discuss the lack of modesty currently on display across the fashion industry. "You see more people who are half nude," said Sadie, shaking her head. "You know what I mean . . . just the personal part of the body is covered, but everything else is exposed. In the olden days your clothing covered your body to the knee."

Here, she seemed to be struggling. Throughout our interviews, Sadie had encouraged me to help her put her thoughts into words, but I was always reluctant to change her language. I didn't want to misrepresent her point of view. So I waited, and would keep waiting to get her final word on the subject until she returned the manuscript.

But that day, Sadie had started me thinking. "I came of age in the seventies," I began. "I wore hot pants and short skirts like everyone else. But I find myself feeling very uncomfortable with the current public display of any and all body parts. I don't think the way our culture encourages women—and especially teenagers—to dress, or appear undressed, in public is respectful. I don't want to see what someone I don't even know—or worse yet, someone I *do* know—looks like without their clothes . . . I don't want to be confronted by someone's entire backside just because I happen to walk by as he or she is kneeling down. And I'm sure my discomfort seems as old-fashioned to my daughter as my parents' generation and their disapproval did to me. But it seems like we've crossed a line during the past few years."

Embarrassed now by the lecture I had just delivered, I waited, once again, for Sadie's response.

But Sadie was done talking. Thinking back, I remembered how Sadie had looked at that moment: her calm, direct gaze seemed to indicate agreement, but her folded hands on top of the table signaled that the subject was closed.

Only months later, with unmistakable finality, would she pencil a discreet yet comprehensive final note on the subject:

"We are living in Modern times," she wrote.

Tony had joined us in the middle of that second interview, providing welcome relief as I stumbled through questions I feared were becoming redundant. Sadie had been unusually quiet that day, but as soon as Tony sat down she began to respond. I had asked her what lessons she'd like to pass on to others.

"Always be truthful," she said. "Being truthful will keep you out of misunderstandings with others."

"How did you learn that?"

"Well, say Tony and I had a misunderstanding," she began slowly, "and someone comes up to me and asks about it. I say, 'Oh no, I don't know that Tony and I have a misunderstanding.' This way it will be peaceful between Tony and me . . . No one else knows about it, so we can still be friends."

I realized what she was saying was important, although it didn't seem exactly on point. Perhaps she was suggesting discretion in circumstances where the truth might make a situation worse. But she also seemed to believe that misunderstandings could always be resolved peacefully. That, in some sense, they never existed.

"Part of what you're saying has to do with being respectful about your relationships. Not gossiping . . . having good boundaries."

"I have to learn this," said Tony quietly.

I wanted to hear more from him, so I nodded at him to continue.

"Our community is close-knit," said Tony thoughtfully. "So when you have a problem with Sadie and someone else asks about it, you say, 'Well, I think things will be okay, and we'll work things out, instead of making the problem bigger and getting other people involved . . . Maybe they have an interest in making things worse rather than better. So you're right, Sadie. Don't talk about your friends or relationships to other people because it will make things worse."

"Silence is golden," said Sadie.

"Sometimes I don't think people understand at all what that phrase means," I suggested. "There's not much silence in our lives. We have cell phones, TV, iPads . . . but there's very little silence. In fact, if you used that phrase today, people might think you're describing the virtues of sitting in a room with no noise."

Sadie nodded her head.

"Here's another example," she said. "If you witness an argument among friends, don't take part. Instead of relaying the misunderstanding in your own words, let them have a kind of cooling-off period to think things over."

Tony added, "It comes from another Arabic saying: 'If speech is silver, silence is gold.' And that doesn't mean you should be silent. It's a lot like the English saying: 'If you have nothing nice to say, don't say anything at all.' If you do that, you avoid a lot of problems."

Sadie watched Tony fondly as he continued. "Because sometimes, even though we like to get our feelings out—even our anger—doing that doesn't always help the relationship. Getting something off our chest might help us in the moment, but it doesn't help relationships."

Sadie's next comment was even more foreign to current popular belief: "People can be quite rude, even when you don't deserve it. And you would like to tell them off, but you swallow it and keep it to yourself."

"Not a lot of people can do that, Sadie," Tony remarked.

"Why do you think that's important?" I asked, feeling my own resistance—a strong, automatic response I would examine later. But at the moment I wanted to hear more.

"Because if you answer them, it's going to start a discrepancy between the two of you, and it might involve others, like relatives and friends," explained Sadie. "Do you follow me?"

"I think I do," I answered. "I also think the way you focus on how your actions will affect the community is special. In a subtle way, you're leading by example."

At this point I turned off the tape, recalling the excitement I'd felt toward the end of that interview. That day I had learned and perhaps even resolved something I wanted to pass on to others. Something personal—but I couldn't remember what it was. So I gave myself one night and two glasses of wine to think about it.

The next day it came to me: Sadie had provided an alternative to the intense anger I used almost daily to navigate what I perceived to be a misogynist world. It was a shield I had carried for decades, and with good reason—I didn't know how to stand up for myself *without* getting angry. And since I had grown up before the term "sexual harassment" existed for the public at large, I had no way to identify or rebuff the behaviors of the boys and men who pursued and intimidated me with unwanted advances in both professional and academic settings. Like many women and girls, I had also experienced the kind of violence that gave me reason to believe I'd need to defend myself physically.

I'll never forget one day in particular, as I rode home from junior high school on the bus. That afternoon, primal instinct had kicked in when a neighborhood bully sat next to me and punched me in the chest. Normally, he dragged girls to the back of the bus to grope under their skirts or blouses while the other boys watched. But that day, before I could comprehend what had happened, he was standing in the aisle pointing to the rips in his sweater, shirt, and flesh where I had bitten his arm with the speed and force of a wild animal. I couldn't have done that consciously.

Many years later, thanks to an excellent therapist and increased enforcement of sexual harassment law in the workplace, I would have the language I needed to name and resist aggression and harassment directed my way. Unfortunately, I had an equally angry response to any kind of conflict, regardless of whether the situation at hand warranted that level of intensity.

Perhaps that's why Sadie's words got my attention. Her approach to conflict required more than a physical or verbal display of courage. What Sadie described required internal control and fortitude. It took a level of confidence, presence of mind, and commitment to peace that I had only begun to understand. I hadn't been able to hear the true meaning of her words until more than a year after she said them. I found myself wishing the world at large—and our leaders at home and around the globe—could hear them, too.

SADIE HAD ALSO taught me about leadership. As a child, I understood what it meant to "lead" in a very literal way. Every time I heard the word "leader" I would imagine a large man marching a line of other men into battle.

It took me another couple of decades to believe that women and girls could lead, too, but I still thought leading meant being "in charge" of something. That is, until I talked with Sadie and her good friend Tony, nearly fifty years her junior.

"I've known Sadie for twenty years," he said, "and she doesn't miss an event at church. She comes from morning until they close. She does things quietly, but she comes and works, and if they need something, she gets it done."

"Follow-through," replied Sadie. "We undertake; we follow it through."

I felt a story coming.

"Years ago, we printed program books before a church election," began Sadie, referring to the promotional booklet they'd printed to raise money for the twenty-fifth anniversary of their church society. "We'd go out to the candidates and get ads for the program book. We sold ads for $500 per page, $250 per half page."

Later, I learned that the official name for the "society" Sadie referred to was the Altar Society & St. Anne's Club, described on the St. Maron's website as an "organization of women who gather monthly to pray, socialize, and share ideas." Part of their role was to "raise funds for the various needs of the Parish and for the poor."

I was impressed.

But that day I let Sadie talk without interruption. "I still call people for donations," she explained. "'Tony, I'm selling donations for so and so; would you like to buy tickets?'" said Sadie, demonstrating her approach.

"Sounds like you're good at sales," I commented.

"She's not shy about asking people to do things for the church," chimed in Tony.

"And I take 'no' with a smile," she added, flashing a sweet one at her friend.

"And then," replied Tony, enjoying the banter, "if I dare even talk to those people, she says, 'Stay away from my customers!'"

At that point, I realized that all we'd talked about so far was what Sadie had contributed. What she'd *given.* So I asked, "What have you gotten personally from being so involved with the community?"

This time she answered without hesitation: "I've made many friends, and I've earned a lot of respect. Now, people never turn me down on any request for support." She thought for a moment before continuing. "When newcomers arrive, I make sure I approach them and talk to them. I ask them to join the societies of the church."

After a pause, she added, "I have served as president, secretary, and treasurer in our church society over the years."

She loves this, I thought, marveling at her zeal for fundraising.

"Sadie takes a leadership role through service," explained Tony. "She doesn't have to be the acknowledged leader, but she's in a leadership position because of her service. So everyone thinks of her as a leader, even though she's not the head of anything. I know this because we all come to her to see what she thinks about an idea."

Another person might have pushed away the compliments; still others would have fished for more. But for Sadie, Tony's comments were a matter of fact. He wasn't telling her anything she didn't already know about herself. So she continued to listen quietly, looking down at the table.

After another moment of silence, Tony added, "I don't think Sadie even notices how important she is. But other people know. The previous priest, Father Michael, told me that people like Sadie are very important in the life of the community because of the standards they set—because they have no problems with anybody. It kind of radiates a 'no trouble' feeling throughout the community, and others notice it. They can't pin it down to anything concrete, but they notice it."

At that moment I realized how different Sadie was from any woman I knew or had met. In spite of her size, her age, and her careful speech patterns, Sadie carried a level of gravitas I would expect from a CEO or college president.

"Sadie's presence radiates in such a way that people feel a sense of longevity," Tony added. "A sense that at St. Maron's we're working for the long term; we're not here for just a day or two. So when they look at another person within the community, maybe they think, 'I'm going to see this person for fifty more years, so we'd better get along until we're seventy or eighty.' And they think about that because they see Sadie, who has lived in the community all her life."

"And started the ball rolling in the early twenties," added Sadie with a chuckle.

There it was again: a sense that I was about to see something differently because of what Sadie had said. What was I letting in this time? Perhaps I was giving myself permission to stay in one place . . . permission to stop darting from one thing to another and "settle down" within a community. All my life I had experienced conflict between wanting to belong to a group and feeling boxed in. I resisted structure. I had a visceral response to joining clubs and believed it would not be possible to maintain autonomy within a spiritual organization. Yet even Tony—a creative, energetic, highly independent person—seemed to love being part of this church.

Listening to Sadie and watching her interact with her expansive Lebanese family, I understood that while no community is perfect, some are very, very good.

"I'm not saying I never had problems," she added, almost as an afterthought. "We don't always agree with our friends. Family members don't always get along. I haven't even always agreed with my priest."

"But you stuck around. You never gave up and you got a lot in return."

"I wouldn't change a thing," said Sadie.

I could tell we were nearing the end of our interview. Sadie had eaten next to nothing—a few slices of toast from my breakfast—and she looked tired. But with Tony still at the table, she had one more thing to say.

"I'm going to tell you something that I tell lots of people these days. Sometimes they say to me, 'You're too old to do this or that.' And you know what I tell them?" she asked, ignoring Tony's surprised expression. "I say, 'As you are now, so was I; as I am now, so you shall be.'"

I imagined myself at age ninety-six. I'd always feared getting old, but for a brief moment it seemed possible that ninety-six might not be so terrible; I might not even hate it. Tony would be a few years behind me—probably still smoking cigars—and my best friend would be a few years ahead. That meant I wouldn't be the only bent-over person with a wrinkled face and sagging flesh.

"Don't judge me by my age, judge me by my ability," explained this woman who had no time for vanity. And that's when I realized Sadie wasn't talking about *looking* older. Her message had nothing to do with physical beauty, which seemed to be all that mattered to me. I didn't want it to matter, but that's why I needed to be around women like Sadie. I had nearly fifty years to go before I reached Sadie's age, but she had just reminded me that I wouldn't escape. The very thought terrified me.

Meanwhile, Sadie was feeling generous. "And those people who do judge me—I hope they all grow to reach a very old age," she added, with a twinkle in her eye.

THE DAY OF the Lebanese dinner turned out to be cool and sunny, and St. Maron's parking lot was nearly full when my daughter, Rowan, and I arrived around two o'clock. Walking through the back door, it was easy to follow the sounds of people laughing and talking. I knew where the dinner was to be held but had no idea where to sit or with whom. I needn't have worried.

As soon as we reached the door, a handsome young man approached, smiling. How many of us would there be? Did we need tickets? Where would we like to sit?

As our host helped us look for a table, I noticed another smiling face moving in our direction: it was Tony. Taking over as host, he quickly found seating for three; apparently, he was leaving his own family's table to join ours, at least for a while.

"Where's Sadie?" I asked.

"Oh, she's in the kitchen, where she's been all morning," said Tony.

"Is she serving?"

"No, she's helping prepare the food. Don't worry—she'll be out to see you," he reassured me. After a slight pause, he asked, "Will you be having raw *kibbeh*?"

As he waited for my answer, I noticed that his friends around the table were watching me carefully.

"What is it?"

"It's a mixture of raw ground beef—excellent ground sirloin—and some grains and spices. It's delicious," explained Tony.

"Mmmmm . . . reminds me of the raw meatloaf I used to eat by the handful before my mother put it in the oven," I replied. I thought of how Mom used her hands to mix the freezing meat with cold milk and eggs, raw onion, corn flakes, and spices. Those were happy times for me.

By then my mouth was watering as Rowan politely tried to show interest and gestured toward the counter leading to the kitchen where the meal was being served.

"Okay, let's get some food," I relented, looking for Sadie as we approached the counter. But Tony was right—she wasn't serving. I would have to wait to see her.

Back at the table, we talked about how the annual dinner had changed over the years. "We serve the same meal we always have—and charge almost the same price, too," complained Tony, shaking his head. "We used to hold the dinner just for St. Maron church members, but this year we opened it up to the neighborhood."

Lucky for me, I thought, noticing something white moving into my peripheral vision and making a beeline for my table. "Sadie!"

There she was, dressed in a large white apron.

"Hi Jen-ney," she said in that precise, measured way she had of enunciating, which also indicated one had her absolute, undivided attention. "How are you, honey?"

Before I could decide how to greet her—should I shake her hand or throw my arms around her?—she was standing in front of me, arms stretched out to receive the warm hug I had hoped for.

"Fine now," I answered.

As Sadie sat down next to me, I introduced her to Rowan.

"I'm so glad you came, Rowan," said my gracious friend. "Are you enjoying the food?"

With a mouth too full to answer, Rowan merely nodded.

"Good," said Sadie, turning back to me. "How's the *kibbeh*?"

"Delicious, Sadie," I replied, noticing once again the bright eyes, strong nose, and pure white hair, covered now by a net. She looked adorable.

"We had a contest to see who could sell the most tickets," announced Tony from the other side of the table. "And guess who won?"

"Was it you?" I asked, looking at Sadie.

"I sold a hundred tickets," she replied.

"Now that I know how fabulous the food is, I'll bring a bunch of my friends next year," I said, as Tony offered to get tickets.

"Oh no you don't!" quipped Sadie, turning to face him. "Keep your hands off my customers!"

As the banter continued, I enjoyed watching Sadie in action. Seated next to Tony now, she leaned toward him and pushed her face toward his. When she cocked her head coquettishly to one side, I could see her eyes gleaming as she verbally threw down the gauntlet over who would sell us next year's tickets. She was flirting! Tony, pretending to be innocent, was enjoying every minute. And I was enjoying the display of deep trust and affection between the two of them. *They're such good friends,* I thought, as Sadie turned back to me.

"Now, Jenney. Tell me how you've been," she said, leaning forward—and for the next few moments, I was the most important person in her world.

We talked about my work with clients, her work getting ready for the dinner, our respective vacation plans. All too soon, it was time for Sadie to get back to her job.

"I'm almost done with your chapter," I reported as she stood up, smoothing her apron. "Tony even read it and gave me his corrections."

"Well, I look forward to reading it," she said, giving me one more hug before moving away from the table.

I watched Sadie walk slowly but determinedly into the crowd. Then she turned, pointed at me, and said, "Call me."

I smiled.

"You call me," she said again.

"I will," I promised as she made her way back to the kitchen.

SUMMER FLEW BY and it was late August before I called Sadie. She didn't answer her phone the first time. Nor did she pick up her phone the next day when I called a second time. A week later, after I'd called Sadie's house several times, I got worried and contacted Tony.

"Oh, she's probably just busy during the days," he said. "Try her around four or five in the afternoon."

I waited a week and tried again. When Sadie picked up the phone, I felt a huge sense of relief.

"Sadie, this is Jenney—I've been trying to reach you for a couple of weeks. How are you?" I asked, trying to mask my anxiety.

"Not so good," said Sadie. She sounded tired and I was suddenly scared to ask for details.

"It's my heart," she explained. "I had a little problem a few weeks ago and they took me to the hospital. Now I'm better, but I'm awfully tired."

When I asked what happened in the hospital she said they had kept her for a few days in order to do a "procedure."

"It's my ticker. I'm always tired and I sleep a lot."

"Well, if that's what you need, that's good," I said, trying to sound hopeful.

"No—it's not good. But I did read the chapter, and I can give it to Tony next time I see him at church."

Not wanting to give up a chance to see her again, I asked, "What if I come over to your house and pick it up?"

She agreed, and we spent the next few minutes comparing calendars. Sadie would be working on St. Maron's annual festival and wouldn't be available until mid-September. But I was happy to wait, as long as Sadie's heart kept beating.

She must have been thinking the same thing. At the end of the conversation, I said, "I look forward to seeing you then, Sadie."

"Me too, honey," said Sadie. "God willing."

My own heart sank as I hung up the phone.

A FEW WEEKS later on a gray and rainy afternoon, I parked around the corner from Sadie's house. As I walked up the front sidewalk, I could barely read the handwritten sign instructing all who approached her door to come to the back entrance. But when I got inside the back hallway, I wasn't sure which door was Sadie's. So I was relieved to see, through the curtains, what I hoped was Sadie's white head coming slowly down the steps. I had expected she would simply hand me the manuscript at the door, and was pleasantly surprised when a smiling, perfectly coiffed Sadie invited me to follow her up the steps and into the top floor of the duplex—the very space she had shared with her husband and son. The place she had called home for sixty-seven years.

As Sadie led me through the kitchen and dining room, I made an effort not to stare or to linger in any one spot. Curious as I was about each of these rooms, I wanted to be respectful of her time. Finally, she stopped when we reached the living room—a large, rectangular space framed by beige and gold velvet wallpaper that she later told me had been in place since the apartment was redecorated in 1938. I sat on a sofa across the room from Sadie, who initially chose one of the comfortable pieces of furniture arranged neatly along the adjacent wall. But when neither of us could hear the other clearly, Sadie moved to the sofa so we could sit next to each other.

I had peeked at Sadie's changes to the manuscript when she left the room to hang up my coat, so I knew she'd written a final note on the last page, thanking me for writing about her. *She must not think we'll see each other again.*

I wanted to find out more about her health before we talked about the book, so I asked for details and was surprised when she gave them to me. She'd had an "episode" and was relieved when it turned out not to be a heart attack. Still, the hospital had kept her for observation and, since her return home, the doctors had continued to monitor her progress. In fact, she was hooked up to a device that kept track of her heartbeat and she was to turn it in at the end of one month.

"Are you in pain?" I asked.

"Well, Jenney, my arms hurt," she said, stroking each arm with the opposite hand. "And I tire out easily."

And then she looked at me in a way I had come to recognize as a signal that she was about to tell me something important.

Taking a breath, she looked carefully into my eyes. Then, slowly, she made two statements I will remember for the rest of my life: "The body deteriorates. I face it."

THAT AFTERNOON SADIE made tea, which she served along with pastries she had carefully arranged on a plate. On my way to the kitchen, I stopped to admire a beautifully embroidered tablecloth and a host of crocheted objects, most done by her, Sadie told me later. A small bedroom featured a dark, antique bed beautifully arranged with crocheted blankets, pillows, and dolls. Vertical dressers with smaller drawers that matched the bedframe stood on opposite sides of the bed, which had been positioned in the middle of the room. It looked like a show place.

This isn't where she sleeps, I thought, wondering when a guest had last inhabited the room for a night. It seemed too lovely to disturb.

A few minutes later, as I sipped my tea, Sadie gave me her recipe for *tabouleh.*

When we'd gone over the rest of the Middle Eastern menu I planned to offer my book club the following week, I felt much more confident about hosting—a job I had dreaded all my life. Finally, anticipating that Sadie would be tiring soon, I thanked her for tea and prepared to leave. Once again I had underestimated my friend.

"What are your plans for the rest of the afternoon?" Sadie asked.

"I didn't have definite plans," I replied, guessing that she did—for both of us.

"Well, Jenney, if you have some more time, there's a little shop a few blocks away. I'm in the market for buttons and my niece opened up an antique shop that has old buttons. Would you be willing to drive me there and wait while I run in for a few minutes?"

I believe not a person on this earth could have said no to that sweet smile and soft voice. I would have rescheduled an appointment with Gloria Steinem herself to drive Sadie to that shop.

Ten minutes and five blocks later, we stepped out of my "isotope green" VW Beetle and walked into an adorable shop. Its walls, windows, and every inch of floor space were devoted to displaying jewelry, furniture, art, dishes, hats, and hundreds of other items used by people long gone.

A man about my age greeted us cheerfully, and when Sadie told him she knew the owner and wanted to look at buttons, he told us his boss was running an errand. Then he quickly brought out a stack of trays, setting them down on a small table.

All business now, Sadie got to work immediately. "Here's what I need," she said, selecting a bright red button and holding it out for me to study. "Close to this size, and colorful is better but brown can work too."

He offered to bring chairs, but Sadie wanted to stand. "This won't take long," she said as she moved a tray between us and concentrated on her task.

Every few minutes, as we sorted and sifted, the friendly man checked on us, offering more cards of colorful buttons. I was beginning to worry about how much this would cost but figured it would all work out if and when Sadie's niece showed up.

Unfortunately, we were done sorting and the niece hadn't arrived. That meant we'd be dealing with the man, who kept apologizing for everything.

"I think we're ready," I said, gesturing for him to come back to our table.

Pointing to our pile of thirty to forty antique buttons, Sadie asked, "What will you take for these buttons?"

"Aw, I won't charge you much," the kind man said with a smile. "What would you offer?"

"I hate when they ask that," said Sadie under her breath at the exact same moment he said, hesitantly, "Well, I was thinking maybe ten—or even five—dollars?"

Sadie hadn't heard the amount, and I dreaded what was sure to come next. Looking at the pile of buttons I knew could bring at least fifteen or twenty dollars, I glanced up just as Sadie said slowly and deliberately, "Will you take a dollar?"

The kind man's face registered first surprise, then incredulity.

I looked at him and repeated the amount: "She said a dollar."

Sadie watched his face and realized she'd have to go higher.

But before I could restate his offer of five dollars loudly enough for Sadie to hear it, she said, "I'll give you two dollars, then. Will you take two dollars?"

He looked at me and I had sympathy, but no suggestions. Then he studied her serious, upturned face. Looking back to me helplessly, he said, "Sold for two dollars."

"This is why the owner hates to leave the store with me when she goes on break," he whispered in my direction as Sadie walked toward the counter. "I'm going to be in big trouble."

Hoping to complete the transaction before Sadie's niece returned, I moved toward the counter, where our friend was wrapping up the buttons. When he looked up and nodded toward the back door, I gulped.

"Looks like you'll get to see the owner," he said loudly to Sadie. To the woman coming around the displays from the back he added, "and you're going to be mad at me when you find out what I've done."

"What?" she said, frowning as she looked at him.

"I sold these antique buttons for two dollars. Your friend is here, and she said you and she had talked about this."

But his last words were drowned out by his boss's exclamation. "Aunt Sadie!" she cried, walking around the counter for a hug. "Did you *buy* those buttons?"

Turning to her employee, she said, "This is my Aunt Sadie. I would never charge her for buttons!"

Stumbling over himself as he tried to explain that he didn't *know* Sadie was a relative, he was ignored by both women.

"I want to pay for these buttons," said Sadie, who by this time stood at the counter. While the befuddled assistant faded into the darkness of the shop, I moved in closer to stand behind Sadie, who faced her niece across the counter.

"No—you will *not* pay for the buttons. I want to give them to you," said the younger woman.

"I *will* pay for them," replied Sadie more firmly. "I don't come into a new shop and expect to get things for free. This is a new business and I will contribute."

Her niece tried to be stern. "Aunt Sadie, this is my shop and I'm not going to take your money."

"Yes you are," insisted Sadie.

I looked at Sadie's stance, then at her niece's. Both were adamant.

But I could see that Sadie had more experience. And so, moving in a little closer, I raised my hand behind Sadie to catch her opponent's eye. Shaking my head from side to side, I mouthed the words, "You won't win." Thank goodness she understood.

"Okay, Sadie. I'll take your money."

That's my Sadie, I thought, overcome with admiration for my stubborn friend. A woman dealing with heart disease who made time to share her home, her time, and her food with me. A generous, loving aunt who demanded to contribute in whatever ways she could to her niece's success. A skilled but tenacious businesswoman who knew how to close a deal and get what she wanted. I felt honored to have been allowed into this loving, unpretentious woman's life. I also knew it might be the last time I ever saw her.

Handing over her two dollars, Sadie packed up her buttons, kissed her niece goodbye, and walked out of the store.

BY THE SPRING of 2015, it had been nearly ten years since I'd last seen Sadie. My own life had taken several dramatic turns, including a painful divorce from my second husband, who was by that time seven years into recovery. I'd also been in and out of a few corporate jobs. Finally, at the age of sixty, I found myself with a calm mind, a peaceful heart, a healthy relationship, and enough time to pick up the manuscript I'd begun twelve or thirteen years earlier. That meant I needed to find out what happened to Sadie.

If still alive, Sadie would be 106. Doubting that possibility, I googled her name and immediately found myself face-to-face with a lengthy obituary. At first I didn't want to look, since that would force me to admit she was gone. But then I saw the photo of Sadie's smiling face at the top of the obituary. As I began to read, I could tell that the author loved Sadie as much as I did—and probably knew her far better. I also learned a few things about my friend: She had traveled to Lebanon and Rome at the age of ninety-six;

she'd spent a lot of time with her extended family at a cabin she loved; her family called her Sittoo (Arabic for "grandmother"); and in 2012 she had died of cancer and other complications at the age of 103.

But what I loved most was the advice Sadie had left for her family and friends: "Religion is first, believe in prayers and saints. Be compassionate, honest, truthful; love one another, share, don't be jealous, and help those in need. Attend and serve the church and God will pay you back in health and blessings a thousand times over."

THE MEANING OF RESPECT

Ruth Yamamoto

IT WAS THE day after Thanksgiving, and I had just heard from my friend Joyce Yamamoto that her eighty-seven-year-old mother, Ruthie, had pneumonia. "These days," reported Joyce, "Ruthie spends a lot of time with her sister, her son, her parents—friends and family who have passed away." Joyce also warned me that Ruthie wasn't able to place many of the people who visited her now. I had met Ruthie in 2003, and since then I had interviewed her extensively. Over the years we had also become friends, so I was sure she would remember me.

Of course, she didn't. When I entered her room, Ruthie was lying on her side in bed, facing a wall covered with photos, artwork, and letters sent by a family that worshipped their "Granny." I stood silently beside the bed until I saw her eyes open slightly—I knew that without her glasses Ruthie wouldn't be able to make out my face, no matter how close I got.

"Ruthie, it's Jenney," I whispered.

"Oh?" she asked, slightly turning her head.

"Do you know who I am?" I asked.

She responded simply: "No."

Our conversation continued as she turned over slowly to face me.

"We've been friends for a long time. I've written a chapter about you."

"Thank you."

"Do you remember the talks we used to have?"

"No."

"Well, we talk and then often we do healing together."

"What?"

"I put my hands on your body and we work together to make you better."

"Well, I need a lot of work now."

"Why do you say that?"

"They're so cruel to us."

I hoped she wasn't talking about the staff at the facility. "Who is cruel?" I asked, watching her face as she lifted her hand to her forehead.

"The guards."

I moved my face closer to Ruthie's. Aside from security staff, there were no guards at her current residence. The only guards I had ever heard about over the years I had known Ruthie were those at the internment camp she had been forced to live in during the 1940s. But I didn't want to be the one to bring up such a painful topic.

"What are they doing?" I asked, heart clenching.

"The things they say to us are so cruel."

I knew people with dementia sometimes thought they were living in a different place or time, and I wondered whether Ruthie thought she was somewhere besides her room. But I had to stop and think about what to say next.

"Where are you, Ruthie?" I asked as I placed my hand on her back.

"At the camp."

It was 1942 and Ruthie was with her guards at the Japanese

internment camp. As tears slid silently down my face, I knew I would never even begin to comprehend the level of pain Ruthie had experienced. "Where does it hurt?" I asked after a few moments.

"My heart," she replied.

I held my hand over her heart. "Is it okay if I put my hand here?"

"Yes. I don't know why they are so cruel. But we're not afraid anymore."

"Why aren't you afraid?"

"Because we know," said Ruthie, her voice low and firm.

"What do you know?"

"We know now that we are alone. So now we're not scared."

For the next few minutes I sat in silence with one hand on Ruthie's chest and the other on her back.

"What are you thinking, Ruthie?"

Her answer surprised me. "I'm thinking, why is God following me around NOW?"

Then we had our one and only conversation about God.

"Is God here with you?"

"He follows me around and I don't know why," said Ruthie, shaking her head.

"When we were at the camps . . . He wasn't there. He didn't come."

Ruthie was back in the present.

"Are you angry with God?"

No answer.

"Are you scared of God?"

"A little, yes," answered Ruthie with some hesitation.

"What are you scared of?"

"He has a lot of power."

A few minutes later Ruthie was breathing deeply.

"I'm going to leave now," I said, kissing her goodbye.

Ruthie may not have known me, but I had to say it anyway: "I love you, Ruthie."

"I love you too," she answered, wearing the first smile of the afternoon.

"Thank you," she added as she drifted off to sleep.

MORE THAN FIVE years earlier, I had been visiting my aunt and uncle at their farm in Cannon Falls, Minnesota—their familiar house sits on my favorite piece of land in the whole world. We were enjoying a last cup of coffee, and I was telling them about my book. I was looking for a diverse set of perspectives; I wanted to better understand what women of color, in particular, faced. I wanted to hear firsthand what it had been like to confront forms of discrimination that went beyond what I would ever experience as a white, Protestant woman living in the US.

"I know who you should talk to!" my Aunt Phyllis had exclaimed, her blue eyes wide with excitement as she grabbed my arm and moved her face to within an inch of mine. "My good friend Joyce Yamamoto is Japanese. And her mother is still alive. She'd be a wonderful subject for your book!"

Within a few weeks I was on the phone with Joyce. As Director of Racial Justice and Public Policy at the YWCA of Minneapolis, she was naturally interested in a book about women. Although I had hoped to interview her mother, Joyce was thinking it might not be a good idea.

"She has good days and bad," Joyce explained, hesitating. "When she's 'up' you'll get a lot of information from her. When she's 'down,' conversation can be very difficult." I was just about to reply that I'd be happy to work around that when Joyce decided her mother wouldn't be the right choice. "I'll find someone else for you," she promised, and we agreed to talk within a few weeks, when she'd had more time to think about it.

As Joyce and I continued to discuss who within the Japanese community might be an appropriate subject, we discovered a common interest in alternative medicine. When Joyce learned I had been trained in various methods of energy healing, she had a request: Would I show a group of her friends how to help a member of their circle who was dealing with the pain of late-stage cancer? I was more than happy to oblige.

A few weeks later, I climbed into the back of Joyce's car and found myself seated next to a tiny, elderly woman. When she turned to look at me, I was startled by the size of her eyes behind an enormous pair of thick-lensed glasses.

I introduced myself.

"Hello, Jenney," my seatmate replied slowly and precisely. "I'm Ruth Yamamoto."

I was thrilled. *Maybe I'll get to interview her after all,* I thought.

For a few minutes we made small talk, and then I turned to watch the road, expecting that this formal woman would prefer to ride the rest of the way in silence.

But Ruthie wanted to chat. "It's cold today," she ventured.

"Yes—I'm wearing lots of wool under this coat," I replied.

"I'm used to California," said Ruthie. "It's warm there. I grew up in California."

She had my attention now. "I lived in California for a few years too, when I was very small," I offered. "Where in California did you grow up?"

And with that question, our conversation turned to the details of her early life. Details I would have captured on my tape recorder, had I brought it with me.

Does she know I'm writing a book? I wondered, not wanting to get overly excited about something that may or may not happen. I wanted to share the lives and advice of a diverse group of women; personally, I wanted to know how each of them had survived with integrity intact what I thought of as a racist world dominated by men. I also wanted to give that generation of women a voice before they were gone.

I never asked the question because I never had to—by the time I got back home several hours later, Ruthie and I had become friends. And I had a new subject for my book.

THE FIRST TIME I interviewed Ruthie, I had little idea of what to expect. Joyce had mentioned her mother's "unusual" sleeping habits, but I didn't know Ruthie well enough to recognize symptoms of what she called her "down" times—sleeping during the day was one of them. But that afternoon Ruthie was alert, her huge eyes glued to my face as I attached a small microphone to her sweater.

Ruthie spoke slowly and carefully as she reached back to her childhood: Born in Calexico, California, close to the Mexican border, Ruthie was eight years old when her father moved his wife and six children to Los Angeles to open a restaurant. When business slowed down, he moved them again, this time to Santa Maria, a small town near Santa Barbara, CA, about 150 miles from Los Angeles. For the next several years Ruthie's parents and the older of their six children—with the assistance of a man who helped with cooking and household chores—provided beds in a bunkhouse, a Japanese bath, and meals for as many as a hundred field workers who worked and picked produce for farmers.

During our interview, Ruthie described her mother as a wife who accepted her husband's decisions without question. This struck a nerve that activated whenever I heard about yet another woman I believed had bowed to undeserved male authority. I had seen that in my own family and heard about it from at least two other women I had interviewed. When I asked Ruthie about her parents' relationship, she said, "You don't talk back to your husband. He's the boss."

I tried to imagine how a small woman who looked like Ruthie would interact with her children and husband. She had been so young when she arrived . . . how long had it taken to get used to a strange new culture and way of life? More specifically, I wondered what it had been like to learn English.

"We were way down south next to Mexico and my mother just spoke Japanese," explained Ruthie. "My dad spoke English, Japanese, and Spanish. He came over here when he was fifteen."

I sat still as Ruthie continued. "At first he worked on a lemon ranch in California, and after that he got a job as a caretaker for a wealthy family," she recalled. "The lady was real kind and told my dad he should go to night school if he wanted to stay in this country. So he went at night and learned how to speak English."

"How did your parents meet?" I asked next.

"They didn't actually 'meet,'" answered Ruthie. "My dad worked with many other Japanese men who had come to the US to earn money to send back to their families. One of these men had a daughter back in Japan; he really liked my dad and wanted him for a son-in-law. So he showed my dad her picture and asked whether he would like to marry her. My dad said 'yes' and sent for my mother, who was fifteen years old."

Ruthie sat back, deep in thought. When she began to chuckle, I sat back too.

"My dad told me a funny story about what happened when she got here," said Ruthie, turning to face me. "He was older than my mother, who didn't know her father had rented two hotel rooms for the night before the wedding. One was for him and the other was for my mom and dad. He just took it for granted that my father and his daughter would sleep in the other room—she was fifteen and they weren't even married yet!"

"That must have been a surprise."

"Yeah, but you never talked back to your father. So she slept with my father that night and then the next day they got married."

Surprise indeed.

RUTHIE HAD TO stop and think when I asked about her siblings.

"There were six children in my family: three boys and three girls," she began. "My brother came three years after me, and another brother came after that. It was Helen, Ruth, Ted, Ben, Merry, and Sam. My sister Helen was eleven months older than me. We went to school in Calexico, and we were so close that on my first day of kindergarten, [when I realized] she was in first grade I just cried and cried . . . then I ran into my sister's room and wouldn't go back. I was only five years old," she said, smiling at the memory. "We were like pals all our lives. We just did everything together."

Ruthie's face shone with happiness as she talked about her sister.

"When we were teenagers we started going to dances. And you know, I'd tell her everything about what I did and she'd tell me all about the fellows she danced with," remembered Ruthie, becoming more animated as she talked. "I'd tell her the same things about me—but one time, when she was mad at me for something I did, she just blabbed out everything I said. To everyone!"

We laughed together at how "traumatic" that could feel to a blossoming adolescent.

"Where is Helen now?" I asked.

Ruthie's voice became softer. "Helen died of brain cancer when she was sixty-four," she said. "When she was sixty-three, she was telling me that she planned to go on a yacht all over the world and spend her money luxuriously when she retired . . . she had a rough time too, you know."

Ruthie and I hadn't discussed the "rough" times yet, but I knew we would have that conversation eventually.

"Did you speak Japanese at home?" I asked.

"Oh no—just to my mother. We took it for granted that she'd never learn English, and she never did," explained Ruthie. "She depended on us kids and never went out alone," she added. "And she always took one of us along so that we could tell her what the store person said to her."

"Do you think she never learned English because she was sad about leaving Japan?"

"No!" exclaimed Ruthie. "She liked living in the US! And she liked my dad. So she wasn't sad, she was an introvert. She did everything my dad said . . . 'cause he's the boss, you know. But she just really loved him. Everything he said was law to her, you know, but she did it happily and wondered if she did it well enough."

That day I projected my own anger onto Ruthie's story. In my late forties I was still having negative, knee-jerk reactions to anything resembling a male-dominated, heterosexual partnership. Only later, listening to the tape, would I notice the acceptance—and respect—Ruthie had expressed for her parents' relationship. I would also learn a hard lesson from Ruthie's family about my initial assumptions.

~

RUTHIE AND I had been together for an hour or more when I asked her one of my favorite questions: "What's one of your most vivid childhood memories?" That day I had no idea how important the timing of our interview would be, or how lucky I was to have met Ruthie when I did.

Her story did not disappoint:

"When I was seven, across the street and kitty-corner from my dad's restaurant there lived a violin teacher—that was his life's work—and he wanted to know if I'd like to play the violin. He had a little one that he had used when he was small. So I said, 'Okay,' and I took lessons from him. In exchange, my dad would feed him at the restaurant, so it worked out real good," remembered Ruthie.

This was exactly the type of detail I wanted to hear about the women I was getting to know: What were they good at? What gave them joy? How did they pursue their dreams?

"I really liked the violin and played all through high school until I graduated," recalled Ruthie. "At my graduation I played two songs that were Japanese and the whole high school orchestra accompanied me. I was thrilled . . . to play at my high school graduation? The orchestra leader was the violin teacher I had in Santa Maria."

Ruthie was becoming animated now, so while she talked I began planning exactly how I would get her to perform for me. Joyce hadn't told me her mother played an instrument.

"He really thought I was . . . you know . . . okay, so he put me with the older people and they formed a string quartet—cello, viola, two violins. And we were giving free concerts," she explained. "Like he'd ask me to play at night. I remember one time it was in a church hall—I played with them and my teacher was the other violinist. Another man played the viola and a lady played the bass—they were all older than me."

Ruthie must have quickly become an exceptional musician.

"Do you still play the violin?" I asked, ready with my next question about where she kept her instrument. I wanted our readers to not only hear Ruthie's words, but to have a sense of her musical voice as well. So I wasn't ready for what she said next.

"No," she answered, shaking her head. "Truthfully, it was my mother who loved music and my dad just let me take the lessons—it wasn't his idea. But I loved music more than he thought I would, and when I kept on begging that I wanted to learn, he agreed just to get me out of his hair. So he was surprised when after I graduated my teacher, the orchestra leader, wanted me to go to his friend's house—his friend was a professional violinist who retired in Carmel, California."

So far I'd interviewed two other artists—Maude and Irene—whose talents had been thwarted or disregarded by authority figures who either didn't see the value of their art or felt threatened by it. I was ready for a different outcome this time.

"It was sort of like a rich retirement community. And his friend agreed, and said, 'Yeah, okay, send her. We'll let her live with us while she goes to college.'"

Then Ruthie paused and looked down. "But Dad said no. He said, 'You'll never earn a living playing the violin, and I can't afford it anyhow.' You know, college tuition and everything," she explained.

I watched Ruthie's face go from anger to acceptance as she finished the story.

"When my dad said that—we never talked back, you know—I was really disappointed. And I was thinking, Why did he let me play the violin? He knew I loved it—and then all of a sudden . . . boom! No more. So I've never played the violin since I graduated."

I put my hand on her arm and murmured, "I'm sorry." But inside I seethed at the unfairness of what was quickly feeling like a predictable ending to any girl's quest for artistic expression. That brought to mind an assignment my college instructor had given our film class during the mid-1970s. To learn about how film frames work, we were to draw tiny images onto a narrow piece of film, which would then be run through a simple projector. My film portrayed a sunny flower popping out of the grass, only to be flattened by a black vine-like plant that emerged quickly and rose menacingly above the flower before pinning the unsuspecting bloom to the ground. When my professor thought the sinister vine looked very male, I told him that was exactly what it felt like to be "held down" by some angry boy or man who wanted to be first or maintain control. I was sick of that. Forty years later, when I remembered that film, I realized I had finally faced the bully. It was time to reach for the sky.

"Inside, we are all the same."

I remember the moment Ruthie said that. It was our second interview; she had been describing the internment camps that the US government—her government—had forced Japanese Americans to live in during the early 1940s, after Pearl Harbor.

"Internment camps?" said Joyce on the day we reviewed an early draft of her mother's chapter. "That's a euphemism. Let's call them what they were: concentration camps."

During that interview, Ruthie retrieved a sixty-year-old poster she had been keeping under her bed. My heart sped up as I read the date—April 20, 1942—and the headline, printed in heavy, black type:

INSTRUCTIONS TO ALL PERSONS
OF JAPANESE ANCESTRY
LIVING IN THE FOLLOWING AREA:

I skimmed quickly over a detailed description of geographical boundaries, slowing down when I read that all Japanese, "both alien and non-alien," who lived within the stated boundaries ". . . will be evacuated from the above area by 12 o'clock noon, P.W.T., Tuesday, April 28, 1942."

One week. Ruthie's family had one week to prepare.

As my eyes traveled down the poster, I stopped when I read: "No Japanese person living in the above area will be permitted to change residence after 12 o'clock noon, P.W.T., Monday, April 20, 1942, without obtaining special permission from the representative of the commanding General, Southern California Sector . . ."

The situation was clear: Ruthie's family had eight days to store or sell their possessions in order to be evacuated by their country to unknown locations and for unknown reasons. They had two days to report to the Civil Control Station for "further instructions." No pets would be allowed. Transportation would be provided to the "Reception Center" and "Private means of transportation will not be utilized." Finally, the US government would "provide for the storage at the sole risk of the owner of the more substantial household items."

In his book, *Exile Within: The Schooling of Japanese Americans 1942–1945*, Thomas James, professor of educational studies at Wesleyan University, wrote:

> During World War II, 110,000 Japanese Americans—30,000 of them children—were torn from their homes and incarcerated in camps surrounded by barbed wire and military guards in what the ACLU has called 'the greatest deprivation of civil rights by government in this country since slavery.'

The profound effects this experience had on Ruthie's physical and emotional health would continue to emerge as I got to know her better. I knew she had suffered, but she hadn't mentioned the connection during our conversation, so I stuck to asking for facts.

"How did you find out you had to go?" I asked, watching her face for any sign that I should switch tracks quickly. Matter-of-factly, Ruthie told me what she remembered:

"Pearl Harbor was December 7, 1941. My dad was running a restaurant and we all were helping him. I was married by that time, but my husband was back in Minnesota working . . . he would stay for the season and then come back home. But in 1941, they took my dad. Right after December 7—maybe even the next day—they came into the restaurant . . . the FBI . . . they had a gun. And I said, 'My gosh, what's the matter with you? He's not going to do anything . . . what do you want him to do?'

"But the guard just says to my dad, 'Get into the army truck!' When my dad was walking back to his room to change clothes, because he always wanted to look nice, the man started following him with the gun.

"And I said, 'What's the matter? My dad's only going to change his clothes!' But the FBI officer acted just like a tough policeman. They took all the fathers of every Japanese family; they took every head of the household and put them in the army truck. And my dad went to Bismarck, North Dakota, to an army penitentiary. Without any notice. We didn't know where they were going to take him. And they told us they didn't know. So we felt helpless."

Without words, I listened as Ruthie continued her story.

"He told us that we weren't going to have to go because we were US citizens and could stay to keep the restaurant going," remembered Ruthie. "So we were doing that. But then they issued another order. Colonel DeWitt said that all Japanese living in the coastal states would have two weeks to get ready to go."

Colonel DeWitt. I remembered seeing that name on the poster.

"We had to sell the restaurant and the house," explained Ruthie. "We could only take what we could carry. We were just like prisoners. We were treated like prisoners," she repeated. "And busses came to Santa Maria to get the families, and we were kind of scared, with army guys walking next to us."

"What did you do after your dad left?"

"Oh, he was in Bismarck for almost a year," recalled Ruthie, "and during that time we didn't have an address and he couldn't write to us. So we sold the restaurant real cheap."

Ruthie went on to explain: "My dad had just bought a car for $1,000, but after the order a lot of vultures came to town and we had to take what they offered—so we sold that car for $150. And the restaurant—people had been interested in buying the restaurant for $10,000 a year before, and when we sold it we only got $1,000."

"When did you go to camp?" I asked.

"It was the summer of 1942. They didn't tell us where we were going; we just lined up carrying our possessions and got into the bus, and we still didn't know until we came to the place where we were supposed to stay, in Hela Rivers, Arizona," explained Ruthie. "That's where Joyce was born."

I wanted to know what their camp looked like but thought a more general question might be easier. Ruthie didn't spare the truth.

"They were all in the most desolate places," she said "See, they had guards in watchtowers, and if you went out of the barbed wire you were shot." That was horrifying enough, but her face truly hardened when she described Joyce's birth. "When it was time for me to have Joyce, they brought me to this building and put me onto a bare wooden table. It was cold, and I had to lie there like an animal—bleeding and in pain—while they joked and laughed."

I couldn't bear to hold onto that image but felt like a coward—all I had to do was imagine what had happened to someone else, while Ruthie had actually lived through it. Compared to Ruthie's life after 1942, mine seemed too easy, my internal struggles trivial. Ruthie and her daughter had endured a brand of cruelty, humiliation, and degradation I would never have to face. The fact that they lived through it made what followed even more remarkable.

Later, Ruthie described how she and her family were treated even after the camps were closed. She recalled a number of post-camp incidents—at the train station, on the street, and in her children's school—when strangers who hated the "Japs" had disregarded or, even worse, openly disdained Ruthie and her children.

"How did you handle that?" I asked, shaking my head in disgust and disbelief.

"I proved to them that we are just as good," explained Ruthie. And then she sat back, sighed, and told me about the women's social club that met regularly in Paynesville, Minnesota, the tiny town where the Yamamotos lived after being released from the camps.

"THE WOMEN OF Paynesville were curious about my past," she recalled.

According to Ruthie, these Midwestern women had never heard about how the President of the United States—their president—had ordered all Japanese living in California to be rounded up and sent to the camps, with only a week to sell their belongings. They weren't aware of how many Japanese Americans had been driven to the quickly built camps, where they lived in wooden barracks, surrounded by barbed wire and guarded by army sentries.

"What did you say?" I asked.

"Well, I told them what happened," said Ruthie. "And I answered their questions. I wanted to prove to them that the Japanese were just as good as they were. I wanted them to see that inside, we are all the same. We may look different on the outside, but inside we all have feelings. We all love our children and want them to have good lives. We all believe in truth and honesty and integrity."

That day as I was leaving Joyce's house, I thanked Ruthie for her time and openness.

"It felt good to talk about what happened," she said. "I haven't talked about some of this . . . maybe ever."

"You haven't talked about it with anyone?" I could understand why Ruthie's friends and family might avoid bringing it up.

"No. I guess I haven't said anything because no one has asked."

I HADN'T SEEN Ruthie for at least four months, and didn't know what to expect as I entered a well-known long-term care facility near my home. After spending the summer with her family in California, Ruthie had landed back in Minneapolis, where she was receiving around-the-clock nursing care following surgery to remove her left kidney.

As I tiptoed into Ruthie's room I saw my friend lying on a narrow bed, her disheveled hospital gown tied at the throat and open down the front.

"This stupid gown," she complained, sitting up when she realized she had a guest. She looked even tinier than usual with so little to cover up her narrow limbs.

"How are you, Ruthie?" I asked, acting as though I hadn't noticed her twisted clothing.

"Oh, I'm tired," she answered. "I don't like being tired. I'm not used to it." She paused, adjusting her top before continuing. "And they want to do everything for you here. I had to tie my gown with the gap in the front so that I could get it on and off by myself."

Admiring her tenacity, I offered to give her a hands-on healing. Ruthie knew I had been trained in a number of methods based on Eastern medicine, which aims to remove the blocked energy that causes pain and disease. She was comfortable with how I was about to use my hands to channel healing energy into her body.

"Okay," she said, lying down on her back. "Go ahead."

I stood at her feet, put my hands around her ankles, and pulled gently, to move energy up her spine.

"That feels good," said Ruthie, staring up at the ceiling. Then she closed her eyes.

Later, I sat by her side with one hand under her back, below her right kidney, and the other on top of the blanket she had thrown loosely over her torso. She put her arms behind her head and opened her eyes.

"Your hands are warm," she said matter-of-factly.

"That's good," I replied.

Suddenly her eyes opened wider as she smiled. "It feels like sunshine going through my whole body," she added a few seconds later. "Your hands are sending sunshine throughout my body."

"And you're a poet," I said, smiling back.

FROM THE MOMENT I met Ruthie I knew that she and my daughter would like each other. Rowan understood more about contemporary Japan than anyone I knew, having studied Japanese through out high school and traveled there with her class; she also had a strong interest in Japanese history and literature. So one day I brought her to visit Ruthie.

The sixty-year age difference was striking—for every piercing on Rowan's face and ears, Ruthie's displayed two or three deep lines. While Rowan's sense of confidence was physical, Ruthie's came from within. As child and crone stood face-to-face, they spoke quietly.

They seemed comfortable with the pauses between each exchange. And as I watched Ruthie observing Rowan's face, I noticed something I knew eighteen-year-olds weren't known for doing. Quite naturally—and almost imperceptibly—Rowan deferred.

The conversation was nearly over when Ruthie finally looked toward me, inviting me with a glance to participate. For the next few minutes, we talked about the summer ahead. We invited Ruthie to Rowan's high school graduation party—she would be delighted to attend, she said.

When it was time to leave, Ruthie and I hugged; she and Rowan said goodbye, hoping to see each other soon. But not until the following autumn did I understand the rapport they had established during their short visit.

By that time Rowan had headed off to her first semester of college. Ruthie had made it through the worst of the recovery period following kidney surgery. And one day as we sat talking, she asked about Rowan.

I told her about the language classes Rowan was taking in college. About her relationship with her boyfriend. I described Rowan's trip to Japan.

Ruthie nodded, smiling, as I spoke. Then she said, "Rowan is a special person."

"I think so too," I replied.

"Rowan understands the meaning of respect," continued Ruthie.

I stared at my friend, wondering what I had missed that afternoon.

"Did you see what she did when she left that day?" asked my friend.

"That day" had been more than six months earlier, and I had to confess I had not noticed.

Ruthie paused, smiling. "She bowed," said Ruthie. "When Rowan left, she bowed. I never see that anymore. But Rowan knew what to do. When she said goodbye, she bowed."

As I looked again at Ruthie's bright face, I realized that one small gesture had done more to cement a new relationship than an hour of animated conversation. Little did I know that I myself would learn a difficult lesson about respect in the days and weeks to come.

IT WAS NEARLY one o'clock on a Sunday afternoon when I walked into Ruthie's room, looking forward to the distraction our visit would bring. That morning my daughter had decided to sleep in on the day she was scheduled to take the train back to college, which was six hours from home. She couldn't seem to get up and I was trying not to worry about it.

Ruthie was in good spirits, and eager to have a hands-on healing. We talked about Thanksgiving and about the weather. Then she asked about Rowan, and I heard myself telling her about my morning, expecting sympathy. But that's not what I got.

"She's a teenager; they need more sleep, so she may not be able to get up," said Ruthie firmly. "I know what it's like."

She turned to look at me and became very serious. "You're not getting mad at her, are you?"

"I'm not sure what to do," I answered, not yet ready to admit how angry I had felt that morning.

"All you can do is ask her what's going on and then listen," Ruthie reminded me. "You won't know until you ask."

I knew she was right.

Then Ruthie told me about her personal battle with sleep. "I'm manic depressive," she said. "I'm doing better now because I'm on medication, but sometimes I just don't want to see anyone. I don't want to do anything. All I want to do is sleep, and I'm mad at myself for being that way. But there's nothing I can do about it."

She sat up and looked me straight in the eye. "Teenagers just need their parents to listen."

She lay back down and repeated everything she had just said, as though she were reminding herself.

"Do you understand what I'm saying?"

"I think so."

"Then go home right now and talk to her," said Ruthie. "I'll be fine. I've gotten what I need. Your daughter needs you. Go home to her."

As I put my coat back on, I studied Ruthie's face. "Thank you, Ruthie. Today you really helped me."

"Oh. Well, I'm glad," she said. "Don't forget to tell your daughter that you love her."

IT WAS NEAR the end of November when I visited Ruthie to do some healing on her remaining kidney. Lying peacefully on her back, Ruthie gazed up at the ceiling as I slid my hands under her back from the edge of the bed. Today I had some sensitive questions for her: I wanted to know more about her way of approaching the ignorance and racism she had encountered repeatedly throughout her life. Maybe there were ways to deal with bigotry that could be applied to other situations—approaches that women who read her story could use to challenge sexism, homophobia, or even ageism—something I myself was beginning to encounter.

"You said you wanted to show the white majority that you were just as good as they were," I began, based on something she'd told me previously.

"Yes," said Ruthie, "I wanted to prove to everyone that we are all the same."

"How did you do that?" I asked. "Give me an example."

"I taught their children to play golf."

I stared at her blankly.

"I taught more than thirty children how to play golf."

"During one summer?"

"No, over ten years."

Ruthie then described how she had learned to play golf at the country club in Paynesville. Apparently, she had become quite good by the time her children were old enough to learn. And believing that golf would provide them with skills, confidence, and a structured summer activity, she decided to teach them to play. Later, Ruthie thought of another way she could help her family.

"I was disgusted with the adults at the club who complained about their kids getting in the way and not knowing the rules of golf, especially since none of them was willing to do anything about it. But I didn't say anything," explained Ruthie. "I just decided to teach those kids. So I started with my own two children and offered to teach the children of some of the other club members. By the time I quit I had worked with thirty-two kids. I became very proud of those kids because I taught them to respect their elders and be polite. They were the high school champions, but they also became wonderful citizens."

Admiring her determination I asked, "Did people treat you differently after that?"

"Oh yeah!" exclaimed Ruthie, suddenly animated. "They respected us—we were Japanese. They would ask us questions like, 'How are Japanese people? What are they like?' And I would say, 'They're just like me.' Sometimes they would ask, 'Are they all good like you?' And I would answer, 'No, there are all kinds just like in the USA, bad ones, good ones . . . you can't say they're all bad or good.'"

I tried to think back to a time when, out of ignorance, I might have asked someone from a different culture to generalize about their race or "people." In spite of how upset I had often felt upon hearing statements or questions that I determined to be racist or sexist, I had to admit that I might have made similar mistakes, especially after growing up in the all-white suburbs of Tulsa, Oklahoma, and St. Louis, Missouri.

"Eventually the residents of Paynesville decided I wasn't any different from them," remembered Ruthie. "They knew that our basic goal was to bring up a good family, like everyone else. We proved that we might look different but we're still the same inside. Those people had never met families of another nationality, so they were curious."

I thought about what might have changed between Ruthie's time and mine—Ruthie had raised children during the 1940s and '50s, before the Civil Rights movement. I came of age a few years later, but hadn't been exposed to racial diversity in any real way until my sophomore year in college, when I lived within a mile of an inner-city reservation that housed a large Native American population. When I tried to imagine Ruthie's world during the time she lived in Paynesville, I wondered how her neighbors might have felt about the Yamamotos at first.

"They treated us okay, but they were not real friendly," said Ruthie when I asked about that. "They always acted a little bit suspicious. You could just tell they were trying to figure us out. So I was glad we proved we were good. By the time we left, they missed us," remembered Ruthie, "and they truly thought we were wonderful people because we never made any trouble. Our kids were something to be proud of, and they weren't snobby, even though they were extra smart."

As a woman, I understood what it meant to have to prove myself over and over again. What I could not imagine was having the nerve, the desire, or the patience to show kindness to a group of ignorant people who didn't trust me simply because I was different.

At the time, I didn't understand my friend or her remarkable strategy. Years later I would come to recognize the spine of steel that supported Ruthie's tiny body and immense spirit.

IN JANUARY 2004, on a blustery Sunday morning, I met Joyce

Yamamoto at a coffee shop to get her feedback on my draft of her mother's chapter. When Joyce handed me her copy I noticed—with relief—only a few changes on each page. But that's not because she was happy with all of it. In fact, she had come with a different message altogether.

Joyce had corrected the factual errors and made a few suggestions. Unfortunately, I had also made assumptions—about arranged marriages, for example—and told a few stories in ways that proved I had misunderstood and subsequently misrepresented Ruthie's culture. As a friend I felt sad and embarrassed—the very last thing I ever wanted to do was offend Joyce and her family. But as a writer, I felt relieved that my decision to involve my subjects' families had been correct. Other writers, close friends, and even members of my own family had advised against that step; most were worried that I was giving away too much power . . . that a family's feedback might alter what I had wanted to say. But I had remained steadfast. I cared way more about my relationships with the families of my subjects—the people who would ultimately be affected by the personal stories and recollections their loved ones told—than I did about how the copy might change. This chapter had presented me with a tricky challenge, and one I would run into again. I also believed that Joyce had given me a gift when she corrected my interpretations. And I was grateful that she trusted me to get it right eventually.

Many of my conversations with the women I interviewed included emotional details of difficult relationships or painful loss. Often during those discussions I would gain a new understanding of myself or even resolve an inner conflict based on something I was hearing from one or more of my chapter subjects. I felt less of a charge around organized religion, for example, as a result of knowing Sadie. My conversations with Maude had strengthened my resolve to pursue what gives me joy creatively. I wasn't exactly sure what I needed from Ruthie but had no doubt I would figure that out.

One sunny day in late winter as I drove to Ruthie's building, I was looking forward to a lighter conversation. I wanted to tell Ruthie about something good I had done for myself—she had become my champion and I knew she'd be happy for me.

Ruthie had moved to a new, more cheerful facility, and this would be the first day I visited her there. She looked exceptionally good: her hair was longer, newly colored and permed, and her skin looked bright. But when I asked how she was doing, she said she had been feeling down. "I'm still a little down," she said, looking directly into my face.

"Well then, we'll work on that," I replied. "But first I have something to tell you about."

Ruthie moved one of the two chairs in her room to a spot across from where she sat on the edge of the bed so that we could face each other. When she was settled, hands in her lap, I told her about the lake cottage I had rented as a writing retreat for the winter. The cottage was located in Paynesville, where Ruthie and her husband had raised their children.

I loved how Ruthie looked at my face—at my eyes—as I talked. That day, every bit of her attention was focused on me as she listened to my story.

"The deal was too good to pass up, Ruthie," I continued, "so I've been driving to Paynesville once a week, to spend a couple of days at the cottage—right on Lake Koronis—writing and shoveling snow." I watched her face light up.

"And the owner of the resort knows you," I continued, as Ruthie nodded. "He says you and his parents were friends, and that you used to dance together."

"Oh yes," she answered, "there was a whole group of us. We would go to someone's house every weekend, and that's where we would dance."

"What kind of dancing did you do?"

"Oh, you know, the modern dances—jitterbug, foxtrot, waltz," she said, looking surprised that I didn't know. "We always had a good time. So you're in Paynesville," she said, still beaming.

A few minutes later, I had a question for Ruthie about a fear I had been dealing with for the last several years—a fear I brought up with every woman I interviewed. I wanted to know how women with different cultural and religious backgrounds felt about certain aspects of aging that bothered me a lot as I faced the second half of my life. In addition to giving women of this generation a way to tell their stories, I had chosen subjects who were seventy-five or older for another, very specific reason: I wanted their help.

"What did you do when you realized your looks were changing as you aged?" I asked, embarrassed as usual by the vanity behind my question. Whenever I talked about this I felt silly. Compared to other aspects of their lives, the way Ruthie and others felt about their looks as they aged seemed trivial. But I knew it wasn't trivial for women my age. I knew for a fact that attractive, youthful-looking women and men found jobs more easily, advanced more quickly, and were listened to more often in both corporate and academic settings. Pretty women typically had more dates, and handsome men got better promotions. But what happened as they got older? Every woman my age wanted to avoid what might change when youth and beauty faded, and for good reason. In a culture that marginalized females and objectified their faces and bodies, the threat of being further devalued because of something we couldn't control was very real. And I wasn't going to shut up about it.

At first Ruthie seemed puzzled but answered the question quickly enough. "Well, when I turned seventy-five I noticed the wrinkles, but I knew it was coming so I guess it didn't bother me too much."

I hadn't been specific enough.

"But when you were younger, when you first noticed the changes, what did you do? How did you feel?"

"Well, I guess when I wanted to still look good I started using creams and different things," she answered. "But after my husband died, when I was fifty-nine, I didn't really want another man, so I didn't think about how I looked. Even then, I knew it was coming—that my looks would change as I got older—so I had time to think about it."

That response was almost identical to those I had received from some of my beautiful aunts. And my mother. All reported that they hadn't really thought very much or hard about how they looked as they aged.

"Women my age think about it all the time," I said finally. "It really bothers us when we start looking older."

Ruthie considered this for a long time. Then she said, "I can see why. With everyone telling you how you're supposed to look and that you're supposed to look young, it makes sense."

I felt validated by that. I wanted to know that my feelings were not without merit, and that the pressure I felt was real. And I wanted to hear it from a woman who had been through the time of life I was experiencing now: middle age.

Then she added, "My father used to say, 'If you're good in your heart, your face will show it.'"

Visualizing my sixty-year-old self with tightened jowls and smoothed forehead, I wasn't sure how good that would look on top of a more wrinkled, sagging body. I also wondered whether the Japanese knew something we didn't about how to preserve youth.

"Did he say it in English?" I asked.

"No," answered Ruthie. "Japanese. He said it in Japanese. But I don't remember that."

I knew I could get the saying translated. But I liked it in English. I liked thinking of a face transformed—perhaps not tightened—but brightened by what lived within a human heart. I also knew that by the next day I'd be anxious again, and searching for solutions—either a way to remain young or a pill that would make me not care.

A few minutes later, as I held my hands under Ruthie's head to help with the depression, we marveled at the amount of information we had shared. That afternoon I had told Ruthie about my writing retreat, my daughter's progress with her school and living situations, the wonderful greyhound I had found after my other two had died, and the trip to Albuquerque I was planning with my partner and neighbors. She turned to look at me with a sudden smile—her brightest of the day.

"You've just told me all your good news!" she said with excitement.

"I guess I have," I said, understanding for the first time how a bit of good news might feel to someone like Ruthie. During the down times she could barely speak; for much of her life, in fact, Ruthie had felt despair. That day, she had shared her joy with me.

ONE SPRING DAY during an afternoon walk along the dirt roads outside of Paynesville, I noticed a small bulldozer moving toward my greyhound and me. Attempting to stay out of the driver's way, I was slightly alarmed when the loud and unwieldy vehicle pulled up next to me. Then I saw the friendly face in the cab.

"I thought I'd better turn this thing off, in case it scares your dog," said the man. I noticed he wore a cap over straight, gray hair. "Do you live down here?"

"I'm staying in the last cottage over there," I said, pointing to a white, two-bedroom rambler. "I'm a writer and one of the women I'm writing about used to live here," I explained. No use going into the details when he was supposed to be working.

"Do you live in Paynesville?" I asked.

"Yup. Lived here all my life," he answered, looking apologetic.

But this was good news. “I’m writing about a woman named Ruth Yamamoto,” I said. “Did you know her?”

“I knew all of them,” he said, his face registering first surprise and then something else I couldn’t quite identify. “I knew the whole family.” After a pause he added, “The Japanese knew how to sex chickens.”

Thanks to Ruthie, I knew he was talking about the ability to determine the sex of baby chicks, which was nearly impossible for anyone who hadn’t been trained.

“There was a poultry farm right there where the F&M bank is now,” he continued, but then paused. “The Japanese . . .” he began, hesitating as he shook his head.

I watched his expression change.

“They were Japanese . . .” he repeated, emphasizing the word “Japanese.”

Fearing that he might say something disparaging, I cut him off: “Ruthie and her daughter were in the internment camps, you know. They were treated very badly there.”

“But there were some . . .” he said again, not knowing how to finish.

I misunderstood: “I know for a fact that they were treated very badly in the camps,” I repeated, struggling for words. What was his point?

“I know,” he began again, “but there were some in town who weren’t very open. We were fighting the Japanese, you know.”

As I watched his body language I finally saw rather then heard his meaning. Judging by the pained expression on his face, I understood he wanted me to know that he himself believed the Yamamotos had been treated unfairly at best, and perhaps even badly.

“Yes,” I said, “I imagine there were people in town who saw all Japanese as the enemy.” We both wanted to distance him personally from that kind of racial bias.

This brought to mind another conversation I'd had with the resort owner, the cheerful man whose parents had been close friends of the Yamamotos. He had told me he was sure they had experienced nothing but openness and acceptance in Paynesville. And that made sense, as my landlord had probably lived near the lake his whole life. The man in front of me now had lived in town.

This time I knew what to say. "Ruthie did tell me one time that while most people here were not rude, many kept their distance. But eventually, the women's group asked her to tell her story, and she did. I think she felt accepted after that," I said, watching his face relax.

Having successfully negotiated the moment, we went on to talk about Ruthie's family.

"I still remember the house they lived in," he said after a few seconds. "It was a really nice one. A two-story house, tan-colored . . . at least it was back then. Nicest house on the street, about a block away from the hospital. I haven't thought about the Yamamotos since way back then," he finished, squinting as he peered back down the road.

When another vehicle appeared at the top of the hill it was clear our conversation was over, so I thanked him quickly and watched him drive off.

That night, I drove by Ruthie's house. I was not surprised to see that it was, indeed, the nicest one on the block.

AT SOME POINT in our interview process I would present each woman with a list of questions designed to elicit their advice. Often we'd get through only one or two topics, and in those cases I'd simply weave the other questions into future interviews. The day I asked Ruthie for her advice, she kept returning to a theme that was of particular interest to me at the time: raising children.

When I asked what advice Ruthie wanted to pass on about child-rearing, I received a lecture.

"Love your children," said Ruthie, without hesitating. "It's more important than anything you can buy for them. Your love is the center of their world. And because you love them you have to scold them when they're wrong. They won't know what's right and wrong otherwise."

Barely stopping to take a breath, Ruthie continued. "Don't let them get spoiled by giving them everything they want," she said. "Pretty soon you won't be able to afford to give them everything they want. And eventually they need to learn to make it on their own."

This wasn't a problem in our household, as our daughter didn't ask for much. It had certainly been a factor for members of Ruthie's generation, who had survived the Great Depression and seemed to feel compelled, as a group, to drill this message into their children's heads. So I was happy when she moved on.

"Some parents refuse to tell their children 'no,' or to correct their behavior," she said with conviction. "That makes them self-centered. And if they're self-centered they won't be liked." Ruthie believed bringing up children in a way that made them feel happy was the most important thing parents could do. "My kids grew up to really like people, and now people like them for what they are. When you raise your kids right, you don't have to brag about them . . . other people will do it for you."

When Ruthie sat back and folded her hands on her lap, I could see that she was pleased with herself. Normally her answers were slow and careful, sometimes with long spaces of time between sentences. She had been very eloquent when expressing her opinions that day, and I was impressed. I wondered what it was that kept her from doing that on other days. I knew her moods affected her desire to communicate; I also wondered if maybe she hadn't felt permission to express ideas or opinions outside her area of expertise, which included raising children. She wasn't like my grandmother, who had felt thwarted all her life when it came to expressing her views; and it didn't sound like she had been belittled like Maude, who had to defend her very existence until she grew up and moved out of the house. And while Sadie may not have been as eloquent as Maude, she seemed to be as sound psychologically as anyone I knew, so "speaking her mind" wasn't an issue for her either, I guessed. I thought about my initial assumption that most if not all of the women I would interview would be clamoring for a voice. Had I made that up in order to get myself to write? Whose voice was I trying to highlight?

From now on I would pay attention.

I HADN'T SEEN Ruthie for quite some time the day I received an email from Joyce, addressed to friends and family of Ruth Yamamoto. Ruthie was in the hospital for observation after having fallen on her face while walking outside the building at the South Minneapolis assisted living complex where she occupied a small room. Initially, Ruthie had been taken to the emergency room to have her upper lip sewn back together. The next day, however, she had returned to the hospital after complaining of dizziness and nausea. And now that two more days had passed without an update from Joyce, I thought it would be safe to visit my friend.

"She's in the ICU," reported the woman at the hospital information desk. "Are you a family member?"

"No, but a close friend," I said as confidently as I could.

After negotiating many hallways and several sets of double doors, I arrived at the ICU. "She's in Station 5," explained the young man seated at the desk in front of me, "but from 7:00 to 8:00 p.m. the nurses reposition their patients, so you'll have to come back a little after 8:00."

As I made my way back to the main lobby and across a hospital driveway to the on-site McDonald's, I wondered what I would find when I finally saw Ruthie.

Maybe she fell again, I thought, imagining Ruthie with a cast on her arm or leg. I knew she might be asleep. And I hoped I'd see Joyce, although on a Sunday night Joyce had probably gone home already. At some point, as I picked at my hamburger, I realized I didn't have much information. But nothing prepared me for what I found when I walked into Ruthie's room.

At first I couldn't see much of the motionless body that lay propped up with pillows, because the nurse was still hovering over whoever was hooked up to what seemed like dozens of wires. When the nurse moved back to check an IV, I could barely make sense of what I saw.

The silent, swollen face—black, blue, and green around the eyes, nose, and cheeks—appeared to be held in place on the pillow by a series of tubes and wires surrounding and invading the bandaged head. Both arms were pierced by IV needles, and I noticed escaped drops of bright-red blood moving slowly down Ruthie's neck from the bandage. As Ruthie's chest moved up and down, another sound drew my eyes to her legs, which I now noticed were held in place by pillows that inflated and deflated every thirty seconds or so.

Trying to take it all in, I waited a few seconds before attempting to speak. "This is the first time I've been here," I said, finally, to the nurse. "What happened?"

She had to tell me more than once: Ruthie had had brain surgery that same morning. She had been bleeding internally from the first fall, and the pressure against her brain caused the dizziness and nausea. She fell again as she was walking down the hallway in the hospital and hadn't recovered consciousness since.

As the nurse talked, I visualized Ruthie walking slowly through the hospital. Then she was on a table. And then a doctor was . . . I didn't want to imagine any more of it. But I still had questions.

"What did they do during surgery?"

"They removed a quarter of her skull to get at the bleeding blood vessels," explained the nurse. "We see lots of these, and normally the procedure takes about an hour. But usually we only have to cauterize one or two blood vessels. Ruth was in surgery for four hours, and they had to work on five or six blood vessels."

Then I asked the most important question of all: "How's she doing?"

I didn't like the answer: "Well, she's been non-responsive since before the surgery and hasn't responded to any kind of stimuli. Usually, after surgery, a patient will respond to pain at some point—that's how we know they're recovering. And by the second day they're trying to rip out the oxygen tube because it's so uncomfortable."

"And Ruthie hasn't done any of that?"

The young woman shook her head. "She hasn't responded to anything. This evening the doctor told the family they may need to make some decisions as early as tomorrow."

Surprised by how little sadness I felt, I put my hand over Ruthie's—her nails were still painted a bright shade of pink. Then I looked at the swollen face before me and smiled. *They don't know who they're dealing with*, I thought. Then I sat down to have a talk with my silent friend.

ALTHOUGH RUTHIE RECOVERED eventually, as I knew she would, she never again recognized me or remembered how we knew each other. But she was always glad to see me, and enjoyed answering my questions about her family, how she was feeling, and whether or not she liked her surroundings. I felt lucky to live within a few miles of her building—I knew the drive was much longer for Joyce and other family members. So I stopped by every couple of months.

The last few times I visited Ruthie, she was sleeping soundly. Often Ruthie slept on her side with her face toward the wall, and on those days I'd sit by her bed and watch her back move gently in and out as she breathed. Occasionally she'd wake up, and sometimes she'd notice me and nod. Then she'd sink back into sleep and I'd wait to leave until she was once again breathing deeply. On my way out I'd find an aide or nurse on duty and ask for an update—her care providers seemed gentle and genuinely concerned as they described Ruthie's condition, and that's all I needed to know.

As Ruthie's life wound down and my own got busier, I visited my friend less frequently. Then one day, after a year or more between visits, I entered her building and tried to sign in. "She's not here anymore," said the friendly woman behind the desk when I asked for Ruthie's room number. I had known this day would arrive sooner or later, but wasn't prepared now that it was here. Had Ruthie moved? Had she died? The receptionist looked at me kindly as she explained that the facility couldn't provide additional details.

Driving the few short miles home I didn't notice road signs, stop lights, walkways, or even neighbors who may have waved as I pulled into our alley. All I could think about was Ruthie's face and how it had softened during the five years we had known each other. About how we had never stopped communicating. Even after she stopped recognizing me consciously, I felt the connection to her spirit. I could still reach her during moments of pain—as on the day we talked about God—or when we held hands as she slept. Maybe she remembered me there, in her dreams; I always felt she knew, somehow, that I was with her.

So when I found Joyce on social media, I was thrilled to learn that Ruthie had moved into a nursing home near the small town on the North Shore of Lake Superior, where Joyce had moved to focus on her art. I saw past and recent photos of Ruthie with her daughter and felt honored and lucky to have witnessed the close relationship between these two powerful women. I also felt relieved to know Ruthie would spend the last years of her life living close to her daughter.

In December of 2011, it was a stroke that finally took Ruth Yamamoto back to her sister, Helen; her son, Jamey; her parents;

and the many other loved ones she had lost over the years. The following April the Yamamotos held a memorial service for their beloved matriarch. These days I can see my friend on Joyce's Facebook page, where Ruthie's beautiful face surveys the world from within a frame placed next to a vase of the flowers I know she loved.

While it's true that I would have liked to see Ruthie one last time, I don't feel sad; I don't even feel like she's gone. As always, I have a sense of Ruthie . . . a sense that she's happy. And that someday, my friend and I will visit again.

TEACHER, MENTOR, LEADER

Hallie Hendrieth-Smith

HALLIE HENDRIETH-SMITH WAS one woman I wish I had gotten to know better; I met her when my life was more than challenging, as I tried to parent my teenage daughter and keep my marriage together. I was forty-nine years old by the time I sat down with Hallie, who had been interviewed many times and profiled by at least a few other writers. She let me know her life was full, and that she knew exactly how she wanted to spend her time, not to mention with whom. I believed I would only have a few opportunities to meet with her, so I didn't even think about asking for more—I interviewed her twice and used my handwritten notes from those meetings to write a short version of her chapter so she could tell where I was going with it. Once she had approved that initial copy, I put her story away for someday in the future, when I could focus on the book.

It wasn't until I revisited our recorded interviews several years later that I realized what I had missed: Hallie and I had shared some important interests. We both loved the South. We also loved teaching. But I had been struggling emotionally and spiritually during those years. I couldn't see it then, but I had needed more than an interview subject for a book, or even another friend. What I needed was a mentor.

OF ALL THE women I interviewed, Dr. Hallie Hendrieth-Smith was the most articulate—not surprising given her long career as an educator. I got Hallie's name from Dr. Carol R. Johnson, the first African-American woman to serve as Superintendent of Minneapolis Public Schools. I knew Carol before her tenure as Superintendent, when we worked together on a partnership between my employer, Target, and the school district. In 1990 we opened Mill City Montessori, a "corporate classroom" operated by the district and supported by Target. My daughter attended Mill City, located within four blocks of my office, from kindergarten through fourth grade.

After I left Target I contacted Carol to ask whether she knew anyone within the African-American community who might be an appropriate subject for my book. Carol mentioned several women, but I made up my mind when she described one of them as the person who *should* have been the first female African American to have Carol's job, had that been allowed.

A few months later I got my first impression of Hallie on a cool day in late September. As she advanced toward me, regally dressed in rich autumn fabrics and colors, I felt like a schoolgirl about to meet the headmistress. Her imposing stature didn't match the soft voice I had talked to over the phone. Furthermore, Hallie had arrived at Redeemer Lutheran Church that afternoon for a separate meeting with a church employee, and had no idea that the woman watching her from the end of the hall was someone she was scheduled to meet the following week. So she was slightly confused when I introduced myself. But only slightly—recovering quickly, she agreed to chat with me for a few minutes after her meeting. When we sat down to talk, I was more than rewarded.

Right from the first, Hallie made it clear that I would receive from her only information not included in a book she was writing about her life—a memoir she would leave to her children and grandchildren. Furthermore, I would never know what information I wasn't getting.

"It will be easy for both of us," she explained with a smile. "I'll answer your questions, but leave out information I don't want you to have or use."

That's how Hallie did things: fairly, firmly, and with purpose.

HALLIE CAME FROM Selma, Alabama, and I was more than eager to hear about what it had been like to grow up there. All my life my parents had raved about Minnesota—the lakes, the snow, the churches with big choirs. For my mother, who had left Minneapolis and her entire family to follow my father, Minnesota was another word for "heaven."

I loved my relatives, but Minnesota was cold. When I swam in the lakes up there I couldn't even open my eyes underwater; I felt dirty when I got out. I hated being attacked by mosquitoes in July, and feared getting lost during a January blizzard—that nearly happened one winter when my father drove us through Iowa at night, on our way to a funeral in Minnesota. The whole North just seemed like a hard place to live.

I preferred the stories my dad would tell about doing business in the genteel South, a place where everyone smiled and called each other "honey" or "sweetie." According to him, the women were all pretty because they dressed up, "did" their hair, and wore makeup no matter where they were going. And when it was still cold in St. Louis, it was warm in Birmingham, Alabama. I loved the South before I ever saw it.

My early impressions were also based on the sounds of sweet ballads I had learned to play on the piano, along with the romantic images I had collected from old movies and novels—images of moonlit trees with long, swaying branches reaching nearly to the ground. By the time I saw the South with my own eyes during one of our family vacations, I was thirteen. Instantly, I loved the sounds of Southern speech when my family stopped in Alabama and Georgia, and I couldn't wait to order grits or biscuits and gravy for breakfast. One year I even found myself a Southern boyfriend, with the most beautiful Alabama accent I had ever heard.

Eventually, I was also forced to acknowledge the South as the birthplace of the Ku Klux Klan, a part of the country where the accents I so admired had been used by Southern leaders to spew hatred and bigotry. But when Hallie painted a picture of an idyllic Southern childhood, I remembered with great pleasure my early, happier associations.

"To tell you the truth, when I was a little girl Selma was one of the best places in the world, because I was not aware of some of the negative kinds of things that were going on," began Hallie. "My parents were farmers, and we had cows, hogs, chickens, ducks, guineas—we had everything you could think of. So I didn't know about all the negative stuff that was going on."

I tried to imagine this elegant woman as a child, racing across green fields and caring for animals. I had spent enough time visiting farms to believe I would have loved the lifestyle, so I felt connected to Hallie right away.

"Sometimes I wonder if that was a difficulty," she added. "I think it was an advantage because my parents were determined that we would not have a negative attitude. And a lot of the things that were so close around me, I was surprised when I was a grown person to know that these things were there! But when I asked my parents about it, they said, 'If we had told you and allowed you to experience all that, you would not have been able to move to where you are today.' So to tell you the truth, Selma was a wonderful place when I was a girl. My parents were poor—but they never said one time that 'you can't have this.' If we needed clothes, we needed them."

So how does that work? I wondered as I listened to Hallie's lyrical voice. What would it be like not to even be aware of what I couldn't have?

"My father grew what we needed to eat," continued Hallie, "and that means everything that grew in the ground. We learned to cook; to milk cows; churn butter—we had a wonderful time. There wasn't anything on earth that we felt we needed or wanted to do that my parents said we couldn't do. You could do whatever you wanted to do if you wanted it badly enough. That's support and encouragement that people don't get all the time—that's why I treasure it very, very dearly and I pass it on to my children and my grandchildren."

Later, when I asked Hallie what it was like growing up with the racism Selma has come to represent to many Americans, she told me she didn't even know it existed until she was an adult. That's when I made the connection between the woman she had become and her childhood community, where parents were able to shield their children from a reality they would face soon enough as grown-ups. By making sure her physical, emotional, and spiritual needs were met, Hallie's parents prepared her to navigate a bigger, often unfriendly world.

The brilliance behind that parenting strategy—one I had never thought of and probably wouldn't have known about before this conversation—struck me in a way I didn't expect: I felt sad. Would that even be possible in this day and age? Every week we were hearing about another school shooting, a regular occurrence that forced kindergartners to learn how to protect themselves from gun violence. Any member of Hallie's family could easily have been brutalized outside their neighborhood by an angry mob. But within her rural, African-American community, parents could keep their children safe.

At one point I realized I didn't know much about Selma beyond what I had read in connection with Rosa Parks and the Civil Rights Movement. "Was it a small town?"

"It *is* a small town," answered Hallie, who said that when she lived there, the population was less than 15,000. Sixty years later the town hadn't grown much in size: in 2017 Selma's population—80 percent African American—was still about 20,000.

When I asked about what it was like to go downtown as a child, Hallie told me she and her siblings didn't go into Selma much. "My father didn't allow us to go downtown very often because of the segregation. He always said that if anyone ever said anything negative to his children they'd have to be accountable to him. I can't tell you what he was gonna do to them, but my mother always said he told her to keep his kids out of reach of anyone who might do something negative to them."

I knew as a parent what it was like to want to protect my child. I had tried to empower my daughter to face a misogynist world by filling her head with bedtime stories about a tribe of "warrior women"—tales based loosely on feminist literature and fantasy novels set within ancient matriarchies ruled by physically powerful women. From an early age I was annoyed by how little girls were "protected" from doing things adults thought might be too physically challenging for them; later I would realize girls also remained largely *unprotected* from a culture in which rape, sexual harassment, and gender discrimination were the norm.

But in no way would I—or my daughter—ever be exposed to the kind of hatred and bigotry that Hallie and her family were born into.

As I thought about that, Hallie went on with her story. "There were seven of us—four boys and three girls. My mother would go to town and buy shoes and bring them home—she would put them down for us to see and everyone would try on what they wanted. If you saw a pair that you really liked, you could have those."

I couldn't imagine buying seven pair of shoes at one time, for seven sets of feet.

"But I was always liking something that I shouldn't have, so I would get the wrong shoes," explained Hallie. "I tell people that's why I have trouble buying shoes today, because my feet were larger than the rest of the kids'—they were long and narrow," she said, chuckling at the memory. "Of course my mother worked for very prominent white women in the community, and they would also give us materials and clothes that were tailored. But I was determined that I would not wear someone else's clothes; I took Home Economics so I could tailor them myself."

That's when I understood Hallie's elegant sense of style. I could also relate to her story, remembering regular trips to the fabric store with my own mother, who taught my sister and me how to choose material and accessories for the outfits we made for ourselves.

"I would take a suit and by the time I got through with it you would think I had just gotten it out of Saks," recalled Hallie. "So of course when our own kids went to school we made their clothes, too."

"Most people were maids," continued Hallie as she reminisced about her hometown. "At one time we had the army, too—we also had an air force base, and many people worked there. But a lot of people worked on farms outside of Selma. Others worked for rich whites, and at the hospital as nurses. The Catholic Church had a hospital for African Americans only; they also had a large facility for young people."

When I asked about whether the town itself was segregated, she said, "Of course African Americans lived on one side of the rail road tracks and whites lived on the other side. And to tell you the truth, the streets were not paved; they were dirt, and I remember the people coming and spraying the streets so that the dust would not rise. Of course I thought this was natural—it was supposed to be that way."

Dirt roads in the country seemed natural to me as well . . . unless Hallie meant to infer that streets on the white side of town were paved. Later I understood that was exactly what she meant.

"Today the house we lived in is still there," said Hallie. "We had roses that my mother planted—a beautiful flower garden, and peach trees, pecan trees, apple trees—all of those were in. We still have pecan trees now. Once my daughter came to Minnesota and was gone from Selma, we rented the house and they cut down two of our peach trees. But the pecan trees are there now, and some of the roses are still there too."

Now I was curious. Who owned the house currently?

"I still own the house," said Hallie. "I gave it to my daughter, but the house is ours and my daughter still lives there. My mother has a different house that I'm trying to sell."

Then she looked at me mischievously: "Do you want to buy it?"

Taken in completely, I said, "Well, where is it?"

"Selma," she answered with an infectious giggle, before launching into details about the housing market there. For the next ten minutes our conversation was pure fun.

HALLIE AND I had both enjoyed an early passion for teaching, so I was eager to hear about her educational background, beginning with the schools she had gone to as a child. She and her siblings had attended private schools operated by Christian churches.

"The Presbyterians had a school, the Lutherans had a school, Baptists had a school, Congregational . . . all those were schools for African Americans because we weren't in public school at that time," explained Hallie. "My mother taught elementary school, and she had only finished high school. Believe it or not, at that time you didn't have to know anything to teach African Americans. But my mother was smart—there were several of them who taught elementary school with the church. The church organized it and my father and the men put in a pot-bellied stove—that's what kept us warm. We had twenty to twenty-five students at all grade levels and the older students helped the parents with the younger ones. It was a one-room schoolhouse for years and years and years."

I told Hallie I had read recently that the one-room schoolhouse was being reconsidered, that it might not be a bad way to teach.

"I'm sure it isn't—if you know how to do it," agreed Hallie. "When I first started teaching in Minneapolis my classroom was thirty-six kids. To be in a classroom with nineteen kids? Man, would I be sailing!"

This topic was near and dear to my own heart. I had completed my student teaching at a high school in what was considered to be the best school district in St. Louis, Missouri. I had been placed with one of the most experienced teachers and earned high marks. But I hated the large class size and upon graduating applied only for positions at smaller, private schools. At the alternative high school where I finally landed a job teaching English literature, I never had more than fifteen students in any class during the five years I taught there. I noticed students in those classes were more attentive and less distracted than those who had been in my former classes with twice that many students. Hallie hadn't had that choice, and probably always taught at least thirty students per class throughout her lengthy career. I wondered why she had decided to teach in the first place.

"I decided to be a teacher when I finished high school—there were seven or eight of us who were so concerned with the learning provisions for African Americans in our community that we decided we were going to teach them ourselves," explained Hallie. "So we went down to the Department of Education and took the test to get a provisional license."

This had happened twenty years before the landmark Supreme Court case, *Brown v. Board of Education*, outlawed segregation. That meant I was interviewing someone whose children would not have been allowed into the elementary schools I myself had attended.

"Our first assignment was about twenty or thirty miles from Selma, if we went across the river," continued Hallie. "And this was so interesting—if we went by a car or wagon we'd have to go about fifty miles, so we crossed the river."

I was beginning to wonder how she could possibly have traveled sixty miles every day by boat when she added, "We didn't have to pay any money . . . they kept the teachers in those days. This particular school was on a plantation, but the kids had never been off the land."

I sat up straight when I heard that—the Civil War had been over for at least seventy years by the time Hallie would have been teaching, and I wasn't sure I had heard her correctly. So after our interview I did some research and discovered that in the 1930s many descendants of former slaves still lived on plantations. I even found photos of run-down cabins, stores, and tiny "schools" that had been built for African Americans on the land.

In 2005 it was hard to believe I was speaking with a person who had actually taught at a plantation school, to children who didn't know their alphabet. "They'd also say, 'I leave this' for 'I left this,'" remembered Hallie. "So that was the kind of thing we'd have to teach."

Like her mother, Hallie had taught without any formal training. "After I worked at the plantation school for a year I decided I was going to get my degree because I had only finished high school," recalled Hallie. "We only had five months of school, so during the rest of the year we went down to Selma University and got our degree. That took six or seven years. And of course it wasn't a lot of money—$25 a month. When we started teaching at Selma University we made $100 a month."

That's when I became aware of the differences between Hallie's experiences and those of the other women I had interviewed so far. All of them had been born between 1909 and 1920, but for them, education was a given. Maude had begun school without a name and Irene had been forced to drop out from time to time, to help support the family. But they had all had access to an equal education under the law—everyone but Hallie. And I bet most of the others hadn't even been aware of the disparity.

HALLIE SAID SHE didn't experience the real meaning of segregation until she attended Alabama State to finish her teaching degree. "That was the first time I knew that you could not go to the [front] door like everyone else," she explained.

Hallie didn't live to see the 2016 national election, an event that seemed to usher in an age of public name-calling, bullying, and misogyny by celebrities and elected leaders at the highest levels—a time when hate crimes against minorities were on the rise within the US and around the globe. With each new racially motivated incident—and they seemed to happen weekly—I felt helpless and discouraged.

But Hallie never seemed to feel that way. "I didn't sit in the back of the bus in Selma, or try to sit in the front like Rosa Parks," Hallie had told me. "I just stood up whenever I had to ride the bus, even if it meant I had to stand up for an hour or more."

And that triggered some very old and strong emotions for me: I knew what it was like to fear riding the bus alone at night—I was also more than used to dealing with sexual harassment, by men of any age. I couldn't imagine having to face racial hatred from my own sex as well.

HALLIE'S COMMITMENT TO teaching was matched only by the passion she felt for her faith. And for Hallie, that had begun early.

When I asked what her parents had taught her about that she

said, "To tell you the truth, the word *faith* never came up, but the action of faith was visible among our parents. They were churchgoers—my mother taught Sunday School, and we knew that on Sunday morning everybody got up and got dressed to go to church."

I nodded my head, recalling teenage resentment about my own family's Sunday ritual. I also noticed that this was the third woman of four who had smiled broadly when I asked about the role religion played in her life.

"My mother sang in the choir—well, we all sang in the choir. And after church all the kids that sang in the choir would be at our house—it was the center for the community, really."

I thought about how much I might have enjoyed that; my father had made a choice to join the tiny "mission" church I grew up attending because he wanted to help the congregation grow. He knew he would be giving up the kind of established music program for his children that he and my mother had both enjoyed growing up in large churches. And while we didn't suffer without it, my sister and I surely would have loved to participate in a choir.

"Of course, we had revival—I was Baptist at the time—and that's when we had a chance to learn that we really had to make a commitment to welcome Christ into our lives," remembered Hallie. "I came into the church when I was about seven years old. And when I first presented myself they sent me back because they thought I was too young. But I returned the next day, and when I had a chance to share my feelings and what I thought, they didn't turn me back anymore."

My grandmother, Irene, had also been quite serious about her faith as a child—a fact that both surprised and irritated me every time we talked about it during our interviews. But without the emotional charge—or the follow-up question I always received from my grandmother about the state of my personal relationship with Jesus—I was merely curious as I listened to Hallie.

"My dad was a deacon, and of course he and the minister did all the baptizing—they baptized me when I was seven years old. But I learned—I learned what faith was all about as I grew and faced those kinds of things. And of course, we were taught to pray; we also were taught to sing. To tell you the truth, we didn't have anything else social to do in our community—I had never been to a party in my life, until I was grown."

"You mean a social event not associated with the church," I confirmed.

"That's right—we were not allowed to do the kind of dance where you dance with a fellow," she explained. "We danced the Charleston, but we didn't dance with the boys." She was shaking her head as she added emphatically, "Nuh-uh. I learned that after I was grown." Then she paused before adding, "*Faith* was not a word, it was a behavior that we learned from our parents. In fact, the church was a cornerstone of African American culture. It provided everything you needed to stand on and to advance—it provided education, it provided insurance, and it provided the Christian faith. Our schools were all private schools run by churches, and every day during the winter—Monday, Tuesday, Wednesday, Thursday, and Friday—we were on our way to a concert or play. At our school, we did *Macbeth*—we were exposed to all that kind of thing—and those events were all put on by a private school run by the church."

"Sounds like your faith affected every aspect of your life," I commented.

"Every aspect of my life," said Hallie.

"It also sounds like your family members were community leaders."

"The community . . ." Hallie repeated, eyes widening as she thought about how to answer. "In those days there was no daycare, no childcare. *My mother* was the daycare," she explained. "In fact, every woman in that community who had a child—she kept them at our house. They just came to my mother's house and brought their children—well, I guess they might have paid her, I don't know," recalled Hallie. "But the community was the family."

"So your spiritual community shaped your life from the very beginning," I said.

"From the very beginning."

"So what does that mean for you personally?"

"Whatever my life is, whatever I am, I owe it to my religious background," replied Hallie. "I have not always been perfect—but if I am not perfect then I know how to go and repent of those things and move in another direction. I'm the type of person that does not believe in dealing with the past." After a brief pause she added, "My children will tell you that if I have to reprimand them about something today I'm not going to tell them that same thing tomorrow. It's finished. I can't deal with the past. I can't. I wouldn't be here today if I did that."

Then I asked for something I hadn't wanted from my grandmother. But I wanted it from Hallie. "Do you have any advice about the importance of religion or spirituality?"

"A spiritual life of a person prepares them for whatever they are going to confront in this world," answered Hallie. "And if you don't have some kind of spiritual life you are going to be floundering here and there. It's the foundation for everything. And of course, you have to know why you believe." Then she gave me an example.

"About three months ago I was talking to a young lady whose mother was pregnant with her when my husband and I first came to Minneapolis thirty years ago. One night all the officers were at church when this woman's mother went into labor. And since no one was there—including her husband—I had to take her to the hospital. I thought if I flagged down a policeman they would take her. But they *led me* to the hospital, driving at a speed so fast it was pretty scary. When I got there and pulled up to the curb, they helped her out of my car, and twenty minutes after she got into the hospital this girl was born," explained Hallie.

It turned out that baby was now the grown young woman who had come to see Hallie. "She was working in one of the schools and wanted to come and talk to me about a ministry that was really bothering her. She wanted to do something in the church for young people. And I said to her, 'You know, it sounds as if you have been called to the ministry.' She said, 'Aaahhh!' just like that. So I said, 'Well, tell me about it.' And she started telling me—we were in my house and my husband and she and I were there—and we were just shouting and talking and she was telling me about how the Lord had blessed her life and what she wanted to do, and finally I said, 'Well, let's call the pastor.'"

Hallie talked faster and louder as she described the three of them hopping around with excitement.

"So I called the pastor and I said, 'Meet me at the church. We've got to come and tell you something.' And he said, 'Well, what is it?' And I said, 'I can't tell you. If I tell you, you'll tell somebody.'"

How exciting it must have been for this young woman to be personally validated by two powerful role models—two adults so completely on her side and so willing to assist that they took action immediately. Norwegian Lutherans are pretty reserved, so while I could imagine receiving strong support, this level of enthusiasm would have been positively electrifying . . . maybe even alarming. Had they really called him on the spot?

"On the spot," replied Hallie. "We went down to the church and had a meeting with the pastor right then. She told him she felt called to the ministry, and he told her what the church expected, and the next Sunday he presented her to the church and presented us as her mentors, and we are her mentors to this day. And of course we went through the process of getting that young lady into the church, and now we're working with her as she's getting her M.Div. [Master of Divinity] so that she can do her ministry of working with young people."

"Wow—that was probably one of the most important moments of her life," I commented.

Hallie's expression went from excitement to pride when she

added, "And during that time she called me every single day and reported in at night to tell me how her day had been. And now this Sunday morning she's bringing the message because everybody in our church has to practice their ministry by bringing the sermon. So she's delivering the sermon this Sunday morning at eight o'clock."

"You are truly a mentor for this lucky young woman," I said, feeling envious. I had always received my family's approval when I did something well, and knew what it was like to be supported by friends and colleagues. But Hallie had described daily involvement—I wanted to know why she did it, what she got out of it.

"I have not always been perfect, but I've always tried to do the best I could—and to set an example for people to be excellent," said Hallie. "I just can't stand anything that's not the best you could do. I can accept what you do if I know it's the best that you can do."

With a quick movement, Hallie grabbed my pencil and held it over the paper I was using to take notes.

"But I will not accept that kind of writing with this pencil," she said. "I have to show you . . . writing with the pencil this way [she held it tightly in her fist] when you're supposed to be writing this way."

As Hallie repositioned the pencil to rest against her finger so that it wouldn't move but didn't require an actual "grip," I realized it was exactly the way my own elementary school teachers had taught me to write.

"I will not accept that," she said in a tone that took me right back to second grade. "I will not discourage that student, but I will take charge with the child and *show* them how to do it."

My own cursive writing was always slanted the wrong way, but I loved learning and doing it anyway, so this "lesson" was thrilling for me.

"Excellence is a part of what I expect from kids . . . and usually I get it."

~

When I asked what grade Hallie taught, she explained that at Selma University everyone had to teach first grade through sixth grade. "You didn't have a classroom, but you had subjects that you taught. And when you went to apply to teach you had to take a test on everything—math, reading, science—I'm trying to think of what they called it."

"I'm glad I didn't have to take tests like that as a teacher," I said. "I'm not a good test-taker—especially objective tests."

Hallie simply nodded as she continued explaining. "But every year you had certain assignments. I taught Latin at one time—I couldn't do a thing with it now. But what Latin did for a lot of people was give you the root—and now when you see a word, immediately you can go to the meaning. Private high schools were the best thing that ever happened to African Americans," she added. "You can say what you please, but sometimes segregation was a blessing—we would not have had the quality of training we got without private schools.

"For example, Selma University was a Baptist school—at one time it would not have had a University status, especially if you had compared it to the University of Minnesota in *this* day and age. But Selma University was run by the Alabama Baptist Convention. So of course, the principal of our school was a graduate of Brown University."

"I didn't know Brown University was Baptist," I said.

"Well yes," said Hallie. "One of the things that happened—what a lot of folks don't know—is that a lot of people in Selma went to college at other places that were connected to the churches. There was Howard, connected to the First Congregationalists, and of course Knoxville College was the college for Presbyterians . . . all our children went to Knoxville College because they got scholarships from the Presbyterian school. And the Lutheran school had another college—theirs was in South Carolina."

I was skeptical until I remembered that not all Lutherans were Norwegians who lived in Minnesota.

HALLIE AND I didn't talk much about her married life—I knew her first husband had been a pastor, and the reason she had moved north in the first place. But I wasn't sure what had happened to her teaching career after she left Selma.

"At one point we were living in Racine, Wisconsin, after my late husband was transferred there," remembered Hallie. "And when I came back to Minneapolis I had decided I wasn't going to teach anymore. I wanted to work with my husband because he had been sent to Wayland Church in North Minneapolis, and the bishop told him to build that church."

I could relate to being a teacher who needed a break. While I had loved being in the classroom for the six years I taught, I was also happy to get away from the responsibility of keeping rooms filled with teenagers engaged for six hours every day. I knew many other people who taught during the day and raised their children at night, but I had a hard time with that.

"I was so happy about the opportunity to work in the church," Hallie continued, "But when I found out how much it paid—and I had this house in Selma and my daughter was in college—I thought, 'Oh my God, we can't live off this, I'll have to go to work.' So I started subbing."

Then Hallie said something that surprised me—at first.

"During the time we were in Racine the teachers here had a strike. And when I came back to Minneapolis they all said, 'Hallie, aren't you going to walk the picket line?' I couldn't afford not to work, so I said, 'No, I just spent a lot of money to move here.'"

Then, looking me straight in the eye, Hallie added, "Actually, my commitment to teaching was so far beyond what the benefit would be to me that I never even thought about that."

As I considered how conflicted I might have felt in Hallie's place, she said, "You see, one of the things that no longer exists is family ties—in my time, whatever one group didn't have the other provided," she said softly. "And that's something we've lost as a community."

She had made a commitment the day she experienced racism as she applied for a license to teach—and Hallie was not one to walk away from a commitment.

"That first year I subbed in Minneapolis Public Schools for 118 days," she said. "And I had to take time off—I thought I needed to go and get certified. Because I came from Alabama, I just figured the people here had a better education than I did—I thought that, anyway—so I took all the methods classes, including teaching and reading."

Based on my own experience with Minnesota's policy *not* to honor teaching certificates from other states, I figured Hallie had probably been right to get certified in Minnesota. But this conversation wasn't about *my* lingering frustrations. So I asked, "How many years did you teach altogether?"

"You know, I have been teaching since I was sixteen years old, so I'm telling you, all my life!"

"But you were a principal too," I reminded her.

Nodding her head in confirmation, Hallie said, "I don't remember the exact year I became a principal." But Hallie did remember how and why she decided to stick with the role.

"Until that time, I had not interviewed for one position in my whole life that I didn't get." In this case, when the district cut back on principals, Hallie had interviewed for a job as assistant to one of the superintendents.

"He had really wanted to hire someone else," remembered Hallie. "But I was the highest qualified, so he either had to hire me for assistant superintendent or talk me out of it."

Hallie had been a principal for three years by that time, but was laid off because another person had a few months of seniority over her. Decades later, when my daughter attended Minneapolis Public Schools, I learned firsthand that seniority still trumped all else. And while Hallie knew she would be hired back the following year, the superintendent reminded her that if she took the assistant superintendent position she wouldn't be able to go back to being a principal.

"I told him that was fine with me, but after two or three days he called me back again and said he had another job in mind."

By now I was starting to feel angry just listening to Hallie's story—this was a perfect example of a hiring tactic I knew all too well. I had been forced to participate more than once in a hiring process that put the wrong person in place when someone at a higher level had already decided who would get the job.

"I kept that guy hanging for about two weeks," remembered Hallie. "But I knew what was going on—he wanted to hire someone else as assistant superintendent—so I went back and asked about the other option. And he said, 'I have one position that I think you would really enjoy and that's supervisor of the Title I program.'"

I was pretty sure the school district would have had to put Hallie in the assistant superintendent role had she chosen it. But then she may have encountered resistance, resentment, or something worse at the hand of whoever it was who had wanted the other person.

"In the end I chose to be Title I Supervisor instead of taking the job as assistant superintendent. I thought to myself, *Okay, while I've got this job, I'm going to finish my master's,* so that's what I did," she explained. "I finished my master's while I was supervisor of the Title I program. I became a principal in the first place because I wanted to be able to make decisions as to what kids were learning and how they were being taught," said Hallie. "I saw so many inequities that I had to get myself into a position where I could make decisions. And I'm here to tell you it really paid off," she said. "It really did. I meet people now and they tell me they're amazed at how much they liked working with me."

I grinned, enjoying the smile Hallie flashed at me as she said that. Clearly, she had enjoyed the accolades.

"But I'm not someone who would say, 'This is what we're going to do.' I'm a people person—we would sit down and really discuss what needs to be done and it would get done. I had a wonderful experience. I really did."

So there was no lingering resentment about why she had been steered into the Title I role—once again, Hallie had turned that situation into one that worked for her, and she had no regrets. Furthermore, her style as a school administrator revealed her inborn determination to address what didn't feel right.

"When I was principal I had one of the first integrated schools in Minneapolis and in the state—Willard School," began Hallie, when I probed about the schools she had led as principal. "And when the district brought in Northeast Minneapolis and North Minneapolis, it just so happened that Northeast Minneapolis thought they were superior to North Minneapolis, which actually had more professional people than any other school in the area."

I knew Northeast had long been associated with an immigrant population that included German, Polish, and Lebanese residents, while North Minneapolis would have been predominantly African American.

"But I knew the problem was ignorance," recalled Hallie, as I conjured up images of the two areas. "So the first thing I did was to let teachers know that I was here to serve the people. It didn't make any difference what they looked like or what they didn't like, because I was going to be fair and honest and upright. And if they didn't like that they could go someplace else."

Just as I was enjoying a picture of this powerful woman saying that to a group of "professional" educators, she added, "Of course, I didn't tell people that, I showed them. And I worked with them."

Ruth Yamamoto had taken a similar approach when she and her children faced anti-Japanese sentiment after World War II ended.

Ruthie had channeled her anger into showing her neighbors who she was and what she was made of by teaching their children to play golf. I would have thought that would add insult to injury, but maybe it felt better for both Ruthie and Hallie to take action that would correct the real source of the problem: ignorance.

"For example, we had an integrated staff, and I'm telling you, sometimes teachers would refuse to sit near other teachers. That happened many times, until they found out it was just silly and they came along."

This woman's job required nerves of steel *and* the patience of Job.

ALTHOUGH HALLIE HAD made it clear she wouldn't be offering the kind of personal details some of my other subjects had provided, I knew she'd give me her opinions. I wanted to know what this seasoned educator thought schools should be doing to improve education.

"I think we really need to look very closely at the curriculum," said Hallie firmly. "One of the things I believe—I could be wrong—but I really think direct instruction has done something to eliminate comprehension from the curriculum. I know some teachers are able to use it successfully, but I think that by the time you get through doing all that's required you miss the real opportunity to help children comprehend."

By "direct instruction," she had been referring to a specific method that requires teachers to use strictly formulated lesson plans and lectures. This approach allows little room for activities like discussion, seminars, workshops, case studies, or internships—the very activities I had always believed were most important to learning because they are conducive to helping students develop critical thinking skills.

I also agreed with what Hallie said next.

"If you expect a child to achieve, he will achieve. If you say, 'Well, you're not going to do it anyway, so fine,' the child will believe he can't do it. Both have an awful lot to do with what the schools are doing today."

"You mean the directive curriculum plus the low expectations teachers have of their students."

Nodding, Hallie continued. "And I don't know when people are going to learn—I know we have all this technology—but we need to admit that kids learn much better when they're learning from an individual rather than a computer. And I think the compassion, the expectations, the patience for the kids that are not getting it at home—that's what's going to make a difference."

That brought up another question, about what she thought the parents' role should be.

"Parents will have to take an active role in making sure they empower their kids to do the best they can do," said Hallie. "Until parents take an active role in rearing their children—advocating for their kids—no one else will do it. Many of the problems are due to parents not expecting children to do the best they can."

When I asked what role Hallie thought our government should play in education, she said, "I think the government needs to put the money out there. It's ridiculous to cut the budget and then expect people to be accountable! Fund the education and *then* expect accountability," she said. "Of course, you have to put in the right people—people that are not politically chosen—and there's nothing wrong with politics as long as it's clean. But if we use politics in a negative way then we'll always have these problems."

Twelve years later, I thought about what it might have been like to have a mentor like Hallie during my thirties, when I was making decisions about my own education. In 1986 I had arrived in Minnesota with six years of experience teaching students who had been kicked out of traditional high schools. I remembered how painful that first year of teaching had been—my problems were so obvious that some of my colleagues had serious doubts about whether I was cut out for teaching at all. Somehow I had survived. And based on that experience I believed most new teachers would benefit from training in a few specific areas.

For example, what if this training included supervised, hands-on experience that prepared teachers to respond to disruptive behaviors in ways that would actually help rather than humiliate the students? What if teachers also learned how to help students think critically—a skill I believed would build confidence and help students succeed in subsequent academic and job settings for the rest of their lives?

Hallie would have been excited about that. Had I known her in my thirties, she would have encouraged me to pursue those ideas at the graduate level; she wouldn't have allowed me to give up, which is what I eventually did. And had I pursued a relationship with Hallie in my forties—when I thought my career in education had ended—she may have talked me into going back.

But that didn't happen. And suddenly I felt sad.

On the other hand, I could still use the advice Hallie had given me about pursuing an education: "Go for it," she had said, bestowing on me that movie-star smile of hers.

We could have kept talking for hours, but Hallie had finally mentioned the topic I had been waiting to discuss. It was time to talk about her personal experiences with racism.

~

BOTH TIMES I interviewed Hallie, we met near the southern edge of North Minneapolis at Redeemer Lutheran Church, a diverse congregation led by a dear personal friend. At several points during our conversation Hallie had mentioned the effects of racism on her life and decisions. But now I wanted to deal with it more directly.

"You've confronted racism all your life, Hallie. What's your approach?" I asked.

"Respect yourself and demand respect by the way that you behave," she said. Then she told me about two specific incidents.

"One day I went to a department store to apply for a job that was advertised, and there were five of us interviewing for the job." I guessed she was talking about a well-known and much-beloved store, formerly owned by a prominent Minneapolis family.

"I was the only African American applying, and the job specifications asked for people with experience in Home Economics," remembered Hallie. "It just so happened that I had a chance to talk to one of the other ladies who was interviewed. We were the last two interviews—she was white and I was African American—and we talked and laughed and had a good time."

I myself had recently left a job with the corporation that had swallowed up the store I thought she was referring to, so I was interested in this story on several levels. I knew the building she had probably gone to for the interview. As part of my job, I had read about the company's history. I had also heard stories about personalities that may have informed a culture that enabled the situation she was about to describe.

"I interviewed before the other woman did, and after my interview I went out on the floor to shop," said Hallie. "When I saw that woman later she said, 'I got the job!' and I was surprised because the interviewer told us we would be notified the next week about whether we qualified for the job. Of course, immediately I knew she was hired because of how she looked, so I went home and talked about it with my husband. And he had an opportunity to talk to the person who was mayor of the city at that time."

I held my breath while Hallie paused to catch hers.

Then she told me that the person who ran that store "changed his attitude toward people after that." Hallie was being purposely vague—even fifty years after the incident—so when I asked for more detail she said, "I don't know who the mayor was, but that person had a conference with the owner of that store, who promised to make some changes. And those changes happened. I feel that if I had not said or done anything about it, that kind of thing would have gone on much longer."

She had handled the situation as discreetly as possible based on her belief that lack of knowledge caused many—if not most—of the problems our society faces. About racism specifically, she said, "I think people need to know what we have to offer. I say to all African Americans—and everyone doesn't think like I think—people need to know how wonderful you are. And sometimes they need to be told."

Hallie spent her life setting an example by "telling." Here, in her own words, is another example of how she advocated for herself and her people.

"Many years after the department store incident, I attended St. Mary's University in Minneapolis to earn a graduate degree. Shortly after I had enrolled I was taking a writing class, and one of my professors said that African Americans write the way they speak."

Poor guy, I thought, anticipating Hallie's response.

"I said to myself, 'I wonder what he's talking about.' I was the only African American in the class, so I asked him what he meant by that statement. And he said, 'Well, most African Americans I have taught won't try to write correctly; they want to write the way they talk.'"

"Huh?" I said before I could catch myself. I could remember actually *encouraging* students who suffered from "writer's block" to be more conversational by writing the way they spoke.

"And I said, 'Well, how were they taught? Maybe the ones you came into contact with were taught a different way than I was taught—I need a better explanation than that.'"

I was afraid to hear how he had responded.

"He said that he had been told this and he thought it was true," replied Hallie. "That's when I told him that I could bring more

African Americans into the room than it could hold who could run a ring around him as far as intelligence was concerned. I didn't mean to put him down, but I wanted him to know that he was way off. And, of course, from that day to this he's been a different kind of professor."

I wanted to ask more questions, but Hallie had a way of letting you know she was done talking—at least about the subject at hand. So instead, I asked her what she thought African Americans should do when they encounter racism personally.

"Ignore it," she said. Then she paused to let that sink in before continuing. "Don't let the ignorance of racism and segregation affect your feelings and the way you respond to things—if you find yourself in a difficult situation, handle it in the way that you think you should. That doesn't mean don't address it. You have to address it," exclaimed Hallie. "You need to call people's attention to it and let them know you realize this is what they're trying to do. And they may not always quit—so you just keep letting them know you don't accept it."

"What do you do with your anger?" I asked.

"You may get angry, but make sure your anger is controlled," explained Hallie. "I'm not a marching person—if that's your way of letting people know how you feel then do that. Personally, I'm going to get inside, where people are making decisions."

Before I could respond, Hallie repeated, "Ignore it. Don't let it change you—it cannot change you if you've made up your mind that this is wrong . . . If you dwell on racism you won't reach your goal. If you never allow yourself to believe you *can't* achieve something, you *will* be able to do it."

Then Hallie said something I have revisited many times: "I just don't think white America can get away from being racist. They've absolutely been trained since the time they were children to be superior. And it just takes experience in order to break that kind of stuff."

"Sometimes you don't win—many times you don't win," Hallie explained. "But what I'm saying is accentuate the positive—think about the times you win. And keep going—but don't give up."

Hallie could have become bitter about her childhood in the racist South. But she loved growing up on the farm, and didn't know about racism until her childhood was behind her. As she told me, "My dad kept us from being exposed to the hate groups and the Klan and that kind of stuff. I didn't know what a Klan was until I was grown."

But even when Hallie talked about the Klan, she focused on what was possible.

"I feel terrible that we are allowing our children to hate so early," said Hallie. "We must let people know that the color of your skin does not determine the attitude of your heart. That's what we're not doing."

I wasn't quite sure I understood.

"If you teach people to hate they will hate; if you teach people to love they will love. I was never trained to hate and treat people badly."

I understood at last: it simply wasn't in Hallie's nature to respond *to* hate *with* hate because she had not experienced it as a child.

Hallie never even saw the hate—she simply rose above it.

WHEN HALLIE AND I got together for an interview, her eyes and smile were warm and encouraging. But her tone and choice of words were often careful—elegant, purposeful, and precise. Hallie had been an educator for over fifty years by the time we met. Her language skills were impeccable. And she understood that anger can motivate people to act. But Hallie believed that what she said, how she said it, and how she behaved determined the nature of the outcome. It was not Hallie's way to retaliate against someone who had harmed her; but she lived her life believing that one must take action to right a wrong. One day, the examples she provided from her own life centered around politics.

I asked whether she thought it possible for politics to be clean. Her answer to the question was "yes," but the example she gave from her own life was anything but "clean."

"I once ran for a position as president of our missionary society," remembered Hallie. "I'll never forget when I first submitted my application, one of the people who was in a high political position said, 'Well, Hallie, you don't need to run for president, you should run for vice president.'

"I said, 'Well, I don't want to be vice president. I want to run for what I want to be.' I didn't get it, and people didn't understand why—so they told me to just run again. The next time it came around I won by seventy votes. I stayed in position for eight years, and I have a lot of people who tell me that it will never be the same."

I didn't quite understand what the lesson was there, until Hallie added, "So don't miscount the votes. There were times when not a single vote was counted from voting booths in the African American communities. We didn't know that for years—they just dumped them in the trash."

Then she asked, "How do you think a man could be mayor of Selma for thirty years and get a GED only *after* he was elected? The person who ran against him—twice—had a master's degree and some advanced degrees. That man finally won it. So politics are okay as long as they're clean."

I smiled at my friend as she added, "There were a lot of times when things changed as a result of action. I remember another time, I was parked on the street waiting for somebody to come out of a building and the police gave me a ticket and of course the officer was very insulting to me. So when I told my husband about it, he had a meeting with the mayor and some of the policemen—eventually they fired that officer. And that happened a long time before race relations became a national thing."

I knew some progress had been made—at least nationally—because I'd read about recent analyses of racial disparities in police stops across the country. When I mentioned that to Hallie, she didn't mince words.

"The law enforcement officers have always been negative toward African Americans in this city. I've always been very careful—I've never had but two tickets in my life. And that's because I made up my mind that if anyone ever did anything to me and I couldn't do anything about it I didn't want to be spit on for my actions."

That made me unspeakably sad. I also had to admit that while I knew firsthand what it felt like to be physically accosted and treated unfairly because of my gender, I would probably never be hated—probably never be spit on—because of it. At least not in this country. At least not yet.

DURING MY CONVERSATIONS with the women I interviewed, I sometimes tried to move back and forth between heavy or difficult conversations and lighter topics, to keep the conversation from shutting down if it became too dark or painful for my subjects. That had happened with my grandmother and I wanted to avoid it with everyone else. Hallie had made it clear that she would not offer many details about her family, but she had mentioned parenting a couple of times and I wanted to know more about her own experience as a mother. So I asked whether she had worked while she raised her own children.

"I only have one biological child," began Hallie, "and when she was born I decided I would stay home for three years, until she was old enough to go to preschool. At that time I was an insurance agent—I sold insurance out of my house for all the people in the community of Selma."

As Hallie talked, something dawned on me: if you took away the difference in physical conveniences available during the 1950s compared to the 1980s—things like disposable diapers, dishwashers, and even car seats—life had thrown similar challenges to Hallie and me as mothers. And we responded in similar ways: Hallie sold insurance from home while I worked from home to write articles for my corporate clients.

"When my daughter was old enough to go back to school, I started teaching, and I taught in the same school where she was—so we went to school together," explained Hallie. "When she was three she went to preschool at Selma University."

I had done that, too—in fact, I had accepted a corporate job when my daughter was four years old after hearing the company might partner with Minneapolis Public Schools to open a downtown elementary school program. So Rowan and I went to school together too.

"Actually, I had three kids—including those from my second marriage. I also have three biological grandkids that are here. That live here now. One of them is still in school. And another one is in the HR area of the Bloomington school system."

Little did I know that many years after our interview, that particular grandchild would become Superintendent of Minneapolis Public Schools. But in early 2005, I wanted to know about Hallie's daughter.

"How do you think your daughter would describe your style as a parent?" I asked.

"I would say she'll tell you that I was a mean mom," said Hallie. "And when she gets done telling you that, she'll tell you I'm one of the best moms in the world."

I asked if she was strict, knowing full well what the answer would be.

"Very strict," she replied. "But you see, I was strict in a way that I set down the perimeter and she knew not to go over those lines."

I'll bet that was very clear, I thought, trying to imagine what Hallie would be like as a mom. In my mind, I saw a tall, slim woman in a pleated, belted summer dress and open-toed shoes—she would have dressed stylishly even at home—with hands on her hips as she questioned her young daughter. She would have had a serious but not angry look on her face as she listened to her eight-year-old explain the reason for misbehaving. In a second image she was dressed for work in a narrow skirt and fitted jacket as she watched her daughter leave for school in the morning.

I asked for an example of a way Hallie was strict.

"Well, my daughter could not date until she had finished high school. And then she had to be home by 9:00 p.m.," said Hallie with a stern look I recognized from my own childhood. "And she will tell you that when she and her boyfriend went out, I had the lights out."

I tilted my head to the side, not understanding.

"So if the poor thing attempted to kiss her I would see it," laughed Hallie. "That boy was a good liar."

Had Hallie actually asked the poor guy whether he had kissed her daughter? I wondered. I was about to ask how her daughter felt about *that,* but Hallie had brought up something else.

"My daughter was not allowed to go to parties, either—that was a religious thing," explained Hallie. "But I heard B.B. King was going to be at Selma her first year of college, so I took her. But after the concert, I left," Hallie said, finishing the story. "I went home and I told her, 'You take care of yourself now.'"

That's a long time to be in charge, I thought, as I wondered how she would answer my next question about what she thought children needed most from their mothers.

Hallie didn't hesitate for a second. "They need to be able to communicate," she began. "Mothers need to listen to their kids. You don't have to agree, but at least listen so you know what they're saying and what's bothering them and what's going on in their environment."

I agreed with Hallie 100 percent on that one.

"And I really think mothers need to make decisions," she said next. "I'm telling you, even to this day not one of my kids has smoked in my presence; I have never heard my daughter say a bad word in her whole life." Then she added, "And I do not speak one language at home and another language somewhere else. My children and grandchildren will tell you that whatever you hear me say, that's what I say everywhere."

If only we had been that consistent, I thought, remembering my daughter's confusion as she grew up with parents who couldn't agree on how to set parameters for their perceptive child.

NEAR THE END of our interview I realized I hadn't gotten to a few of the questions I had added for a very specific reason: I was having trouble with these areas in my own life, so I wanted to know what Hallie had to say about them. We were almost out of time, but I needn't have worried; as usual, Hallie was concise in her response to each word I asked her to address. And that's all I had to do: mention the word.

The first one was "children."

"I believe that if you expose a child to negative things they will grow up negative," began Hallie. "But if you expose them to the positive things, then when they face the negative they'll know how to act. For example, I'm glad I didn't know about racism as a child because I would have hated the leaders and I don't have time to hate them. I wouldn't have known they were racist because of ignorance—a lot of those people who were placed in positions to be hateful and mean were the most unlearned, ignorant people in the whole city."

That sounded right.

"I also think it's important to make education a priority. My children had to go to school. They had to get their work done. They could not play sports unless they made A's. That was required—they had to take music, they were in drama, they had to do theater, they had to do all those things. And once they did all that they could play football, baseball, anything they liked."

Then she looked at me with a level of directness I was getting used to: "But this was first—their education. And consequently, they are all college graduates."

As I wrote furiously, she ended the conversation with one last comment: "It's interesting, because my daughter said, 'Oh, I'm not going to do that when my children grow up.'"

So, *did* she? I asked, looking up.

"She did," said Hallie with a slow smile.

The next word was "compromise."

"One of the things I do not like is compromising your standards; don't compromise your values for anybody," began Hallie. "I was taught that from my youth, and as I grew older and experienced obstacles in my way I learned to use them. My parents always said, 'You're special; God don't make any junk.' What they meant was, you're important no matter what anyone says or how anybody looks at you sideways because you're a different color. You know you're important, so press on."

I enjoyed the example Hallie offered next. "As the wife of a pastor, I did what I wanted to do, in spite of other people's expectations. This is a minor thing, but most of the pastors' wives were sitting around with dark clothes on all the time and stuff," remembered Hallie, "but I came around with a red dress on. And I told them, 'A pastor's wife is just a wife.'"

As my own smile widened, she added, "I do feel like a pastor's wife is supposed to set an example. I don't have a problem with that—but you're not gonna tell me what I'm supposed to wear or what kind of car I'm gonna drive and what I'm gonna eat . . . uh-uh. My standards were set in my life before I became a grown person, and I continue to advance those structures and that kind of character. I did not take on new standards, and everyone knows that about me."

Admiring the beautiful outfit Hallie wore that day I could only nod. "I'm sure they do," I said.

I asked next about mentoring.

"You've got to be an example," said Hallie without hesitation. "I tell women all the time that there are two words I use extensively: Be and Let. Be what you are; let your work and what you do speak for itself," said Hallie. "If you try to tell people what to do, they may not listen. And if they don't, move on and tell the next person. You can't save the world, so you save the ones you come in contact with."

Then she added, "Show versus tell because people might not listen—showing lets them know it will be done. Actions speak louder than words. No one is perfect, but we all have to keep trying."

"So whom did you mentor?" I asked.

"Mentoring a principal after I retired was one of the things I can say was something I really enjoyed," replied Hallie. "And I preferred to start with a principal's first assignment. That way you're with them for three years and walk them through all of the necessities in order to be a good principal. Especially people skills—how to deal with parents and how to deal with diversity. A lot of people don't know how to deal with diversity."

Those were some very lucky people, I thought.

"Going to St. Mary's University to get my doctorate degree was one of the greatest things I could ever do because I had an opportunity to show a lot of people who had never seen a black person close up that there were some very wonderful people in the world—who were even more wonderful than they were."

I could only imagine how far ahead of the class Hallie would have been by the time she attended St. Mary's.

Referring to the incident she had described earlier, she said, "I've never been a person who challenged you all the time unless I have to . . . but to be there and in a position to show what was possible was just awesome."

Listening to Hallie that day, I thought once again about how beneficial it would have been to be able to watch someone like her—to have a role model who combined a strong presence with firm, soft-spoken, but absolute authority. I knew she had made her students feel safe—just like I felt safe in her presence. Hearing her voice thirteen years later made me feel safe all over again.

But that day I wanted to mention something else. "Of course you know Carol Johnson also thinks of you as a mentor," I said. "Didn't I mention what she said about you . . . that in your day, if it had been possible, you would have been the first female African American superintendent of Minneapolis Public Schools. That's why I chose you for a subject!"

"But I didn't want to be superintendent," argued Hallie.

"I know, but Carol said you would have been if you could have had the chance," I countered.

"But I like working in areas where I can make a difference," explained Hallie. "When I'm in a school, believe it or not I'm there every day at 7:00 a.m. And when school opens, I'm in the classroom."

I noticed her switch to present tense.

"Of course you have to evaluate teachers. And I let teachers know when I'm going to evaluate them—I can set up a conference. But otherwise, don't be surprised when I'm in your classroom."

"Well, why do think Carol named you as a mentor?" I asked.

"I have no idea—I really don't. And I don't know why people really love me, because I expect so much of people and I'm just me. I have no idea . . . my husband tells me all the time I'm the type of person who likes to make other people feel proud of themselves. And then they feel proud of themselves, and when they do, I think I have made a contribution."

"I believe any teacher who truly loves the profession feels that way," I said. "Seeing others succeed is what motivates us," I added, suddenly missing the profession. My last year of teaching had been a little more stressful because I had switched to a new school, but

I had still loved watching my students blossom in the ways children do when allowed to truly explore their ideas and think critically together. And while I know I was respected for the expertise I brought working with troubled teenagers, I couldn't shake the insecurity I felt at any new job. If I had worked with someone like Hallie, that year at my second school might have been different. I might have even stuck with the profession, in spite of the obstacles I faced moving from Missouri to Minnesota.

Bringing me back to the present, Hallie added, "I have a song that I sing that goes like this: 'If I can help someone as I pass this way, then my living will not be in vain.' I don't have the slightest idea. I just like to help."

"Well, and people just gravitate to you," I added.

"Maybe," she said with a smile. Of course, she knew I was right.

The last thing I wanted to know was who some of her mentors were.

"Oh my—my Latin teacher, Mrs. Prichard," began Hallie. "My elementary teacher, Mrs. Skinner. My mother. My father."

What had she gotten from them?

"I heard the message that if anybody can do it, you can do it," said Hallie slowly. "And I can give you an example that expressed what I'm saying. My father used to say, 'I don't want you to start down here to achieve or do whatever you want to do. I've been there; I want you to get on my shoulders and grow.'"

When she saw my frown, she added, "And for a long time I didn't understand what he was talking about. I think what he wanted to say was, 'You don't have to do the same things I do in order to be successful. I've told you about those. Now you take those things and use them for learning the foundation so you can grow.'"

I had never thought about that perspective; Hallie's parents had been thoughtful and deliberate about building their children's confidence and sense of emotional security. As I listened to Hallie, I couldn't think of a greater gift.

"These people taught us that we can do anything," said Hallie. "That's the best way I know how to explain it."

Then she added, "I never shall forget Mrs. Skinner—she expected so much of us. She expected us to get our lesson done every day. And my mother expected us to be clean every day. In that day we wore uniforms—and you only had two. But you laundered that one at night and it was spic and span the next day when you put it on."

What a different life, I thought, remembering how my mother did every stitch of my laundry as I was growing up.

"Oh, I could just name you any number of people who were important in my family," continued Hallie. "My husband—I tell you, it's one of the best things in the world that ever happened to me when I married this man that I'm married to now."

"He seemed very nice on the phone," I remembered aloud.

"Well, he's a wonderful person," said Hallie. "You see, his wife died. And I was already a widow; we were in the same church, both of us teaching Bible class. And that's how we met, because we were trying to connect him to some other women in the church."

When she noticed my expression, Hallie laughed and said, "Well, he's shorter than I am, and I always said that I would never marry anyone who was shorter than I am. But we fell in love with each other. And we've been married twenty-one years."

"Lucky man," I said, as Hallie collected her things before saying goodbye. When Hallie walked away, I'm sure I believed I would see her again, although I didn't know when—she was one of several women I was interviewing, and I knew I'd have to start on her chapter before I had more questions. I had plenty of notes and two sides of a micro-cassette for reference. But I wasn't wise enough at the time to pursue a relationship with the one woman, besides my mother, who could have helped me through some of the difficult years ahead. I could have used some parenting advice; I would have loved to exchange ideas about the future of education, and what she had learned as a principal; who knows, I may have even had fun attending church with this gregarious, inspired woman.

I didn't know that would be the last time I ever laid eyes on Hallie. And I wouldn't take advantage of her wisdom until years later, after she was gone.

HALLIE WAS THE only woman I interviewed whose family had not been involved in editing her chapter. By the time I finished I had lost track of Carol Johnson, but there was one other person I could try to contact. I knew Hallie's granddaughter, Bernadeia Johnson, had left her job as Superintendent of Minneapolis Public Schools to care for her grandparents. As both granddaughter and caretaker, no one understood Hallie better.

The day we met in person, Bernadeia generously offered to provide details Hallie hadn't included. But a few weeks later, when she called back to discuss the particulars, she had changed her mind.

"My grandmother was a very private person," began Bernadeia apologetically.

I knew where this was going.

"She was so *proper*," Bernadeia said with a sigh. "And I think she loved the persona she had created for herself as The Grandmother, which was how we all referred to her."

I laughed aloud at how well that title fit the formidable woman I knew.

"So while I believe I could add details, I don't think she would want that," said Bernadeia.

On the other end of the line, I nodded silently as she continued. "She was so private that it took forever for her to even tell us her age—her own family didn't know! And when she announced that she was marrying her second husband, we were completely surprised by that, too!"

"I'm sorry to be laughing so much," I said.

"No! It IS funny!" agreed Bernadeia. "We didn't even know they were dating, and all Grandmother said in her own defense was, 'What's the point, it happened, it is what it is.'"

"Somehow that doesn't surprise me," I said.

"My grandmother also set the standards for all of us to live up to," explained Bernadeia. "For example, when Hallie thought my sister's boyfriend didn't have enough 'get up and go,' she told him he couldn't marry my sister. 'Either you marry her or break up,' my grandmother said to that poor guy."

"So what did he do?"

"They got married the next summer, of course!" exclaimed Bernadeia. "Whether the timing was right for them or not. When my grandmother told you to do something, you did it. Her word was the law. And here's another example that has to do with my own marriage," continued Bernadeia. "My husband—then fiancé—and I were engaged and living apart, but we had to put a deposit down one month early because we couldn't move into the apartment right away. I wanted to move in and live there by myself for a month before we got married, but Grandmother wouldn't hear of it."

"What was the problem?" I asked, not sure why that arrangement wouldn't seem appropriate, even to Hallie.

"She must have thought he was going to stay there anyway, and she went on and on about it so much that I didn't do it."

Bernadeia told me Hallie referred to people who lived together before marriage as being "common." "I can tell those two are common," Hallie once said of a young couple who attended dinner at her house one Sunday afternoon. "I think young ladies should hold themselves to a higher standard."

That day Bernadeia's stories brought her grandmother back to me—a woman I had fallen for after only two interviews. I had loved the way Hallie looked and talked; I also loved her wisdom, as well as her willingness to share it. With Hallie, there was never any doubt about who was in charge, whose opinions mattered, or who would set the standards—I loved that, too.

This well-spoken, passionate woman had earned every accolade she clearly enjoyed throughout her life. I felt grateful to have been allowed into her world.

When I stopped seeing my mother through the eyes of a child, I saw the woman who helped me give birth to myself.

—Nancy Friday

SONGBIRD

Edith Egertson

ONE HOT DAY during the summer of 1935, Minneapolis traffic rushed past the Northland Creamery as six-year-old Edith Fristedt stood near the alley on the south side of Twenty-Eighth Street. The child nicknamed "Itsy" knew better than to cross Twenty-Eighth without a parent or one of her three sisters. But when an older boy from the neighborhood threw a ball across the street, she didn't think twice about accepting his challenge to retrieve it. Ignoring the rules, she ran into the street—and made it safely across. That emboldened the little girl to try again, darting between parked cars as she made her way back to the other side. But this time Itsy wasn't so lucky. While she doesn't remember the impact of the car that struck her, she does recall being held by a Northland Creamery employee, who carried her tiny body away from the accident. Her next memory is of being at home, where a neighbor carefully cut off Itsy's brand new sandals before the ambulance arrived to take her to the hospital.

The next day, an article about the accident featuring a photo of Edith Fristedt appeared on the front page of the *Star Tribune*,

Fourth of July edition. While Itsy's broken leg healed eventually, the emotional impact has lingered for more than eighty years.

~

IF YOU HAD met Edith at any point in her life, you would have guessed her to be ten to fifteen years younger than her actual age. At eighty-five, her wide and impossibly blue eyes were still clear and intelligent as she watched the world intently through metal, purple-toned glasses. Her skin was just beginning to wrinkle around her eyes and mouth. The straight, dark brown hair that always sprang stubbornly and abundantly from her head had only recently thinned and softened, becoming more white than gray. My mother looked more like a seventy-five-year-old.

But even then, standing five feet, three inches in her stocking feet, only her knees and hips, which she began replacing in her sixties, betrayed her age. While two of the three surgeries improved her mobility, one knee remained stiff and uncompromising, causing her to move slowly between the places she found to sit or stand comfortably.

One evening, at the end of a family event, she looked at me with such deep and unconditional love I had to fight back tears. I will never forget that look. But it may be her strong and capable hands I love most—the gentlest hands I will ever know. My whole life I've watched them fly across the piano as she played "Clare de Lune." The same hands pinned endless hems along the bottoms of the beautiful dresses she made for my sister and me, and when I was old enough to sew, they showed me how to create and produce my own fashions. Then, when my daughter was born, my mother's hands skillfully demonstrated how to bathe this tiny new being. These days, the calico cat that runs away from everyone else shadows Edith, because only my mother knows how to touch her skittish pet.

Gentleness is part of Edith's nature. She says she learned how to parent by watching *her* mother—a woman who had been dead for well over forty years before I asked about the details of their relationship. In fact, I didn't decide to interview my mother until I had been working on my book for nearly thirteen years. It took me that long to finally realize I wouldn't fully understand my purpose in writing it until I had incorporated the most authoritative voice in my own life. Over the years I had gained a stronger sense of myself as a writer and as a woman. My work with the other women had strengthened my voice. Now I just needed to give myself permission to actually finish what I had begun. So I took my mother to a beautiful B&B in Ste. Genevieve, Missouri, where we could eat, drink wine, and have hours of uninterrupted time to collect and assemble her story.

THE DAY WE drove to Ste. Genevieve, temperatures rose into the eighties. It was early October, and I meant to savor every moment I could of Missouri's long, languorous autumn. With two hours to go before check-in, Mom and I headed straight for the in-town winery.

Born to Joseph and Beth Fristedt on November 26, 1929, Edith Norma was the youngest of their four daughters. She adored her father, the man who nicknamed his youngest child Itsy Bitsy. Quiet by nature, she explained, "My dad and I didn't have long conversations. Two of my older sisters were closer to him that way. But I knew he loved me."

Her relationship with her mother was more complicated. "I must have been very close to her," Mom began. "I never thought about it when I was growing up, but I know my mother was there. I was the youngest, so I never felt anything other than trust and love, although we didn't talk about love."

I asked my mother how she thought Beth would have described her youngest daughter as a child. "Well, she would probably have said I was easygoing but not very open to suggestions," my mother replied. "She knew I didn't want her to help me, especially with things like piano."

Suddenly I understood where my own low tolerance for assistance with tasks might have originated.

"As a child I was free," she continued. "We lived between Twenty-Eighth and Twenty-ninth Street on Nicollet Avenue—a busy part of town. I remember crossing Twenty-Eighth Street to walk north to a little Jewish grocery store where they had penny candy. Then came Gerber's cleaners, a gas station, and Simpson Methodist Church. To the south was Lake Street, and we were able to walk from our house way down to Fortieth or Fiftieth."

"Weren't you scared to be outside alone?" I asked, disturbed by the thought of a child wandering around that same area now.

"Well, there were street lights on the corners of Twenty-Eighth and Nicollet," my mother explained, "and the street car ran in front of our house for all those years. But I had no fear—I trusted people and I knew they probably recognized me." She paused, then added, "I was independent as a child—but 'independent' may mean something different now. To me it meant having the freedom to do what I wanted but knowing I had boundaries. With three older sisters, I knew what was expected of us; I also knew Mom and Dad would be there when I got home—my dad was home a lot."

"So you felt pretty secure," I offered.

"Yes. I was not a talkative child, but I never had the feeling of being intimidated; it wasn't necessary to do a lot of talking anyway," she said. "We didn't do a lot of discussing with our parents. My older sisters had more going on with Mother and Daddy than I did, so I learned to listen more than anything else." That made sense to me, as two of my aunts were clearly more outspoken than my mom.

"I looked up to my sisters, but they didn't take care of me unless they had to," recalled my mother. "They would walk ahead of me when we went to the grocery store or piano lessons so I wasn't really part of their group."

"I guess that's pretty typical," I said, recalling how I felt about being responsible for my own sister when she was little. I also imagined how being left out might affect a small child.

"I only spent time with my sisters when we sang together. I didn't even play with them," continued my mother. "Really, I was alone for many years, because there were no other girls to play with in our neighborhood."

"What about school?" I asked. "What were you like as a student?"

"I was very passive in school," she answered.

When I raised my eyebrows she added, "I was afraid to answer questions because I didn't want to be caught not knowing or saying the wrong thing. I guess at that age I already had a feeling of not being sharp enough."

"Where do you think that came from?"

"Being the youngest of four, I always looked up to my three sisters. Glenda was very bright and witty and always got the great marks. And we weren't ever praised in those days you didn't hear praise."

"So the lack of praise and having a really smart sister gave you the idea you weren't very bright?" I paraphrased.

"Maybe that was it," said my mom. "Besides, I was silly in class. One time when we were reading a book out loud I kept laughing at one part and got punished for it."

"I did that too," I said, describing the first day of tenth grade world history class. "When I turned around to look at the boy sitting behind me, he and I both started giggling uncontrollably. At one point, even the teacher started laughing."

"That sounds familiar," said Mom. "I giggled a lot, and not only in class. Things just seemed to tickle me—and they still do. I was always the one who started the laughing among my sisters, and then they would join in."

"That happens to me, too," I commented. "But did your teachers help you with your work?"

"I think I may have been kind of flighty," she remembered, "so they didn't give me academic help, and I never asked for it. I wasn't used to asking for help at home, so I wouldn't have thought to get help at school."

"Well, it wouldn't have hurt for any one of them to notice you needed some attention," I said in her defense. I was noticing how she took the blame for everything bad that had happened in her life.

"Were you exposed to a lot of anger in your house?" I asked, thinking of the alcoholic relationships within my own life.

"Oh no, I never experienced any anger directed toward me," answered my mother. "I don't remember anger in our house. I never even heard my parents argue."

"So there you were, believing you weren't as talented as your older sisters . . . and not feeling successful in school either. I wonder how that happened," I said.

"I know Glenda used to tease me a lot. One time she had me pose for pictures and then laughed hysterically when I realized there was no film in the camera. I adored her and she could always make me laugh, but I didn't trust her after that." After a long pause she continued, "But I always wanted to read and would walk by myself to the library to look at the books, even though no one ever read to me."

"You read to us every day when we were little," I said, thinking of the beautiful storybooks we would look at together as I sat next to my mother. Sometimes my brother sat on the other side; when I was a little older, my sister took his place. And once my younger brother was old enough to go to the library, my mother would drive all of us there every three weeks. I grew up loving books.

As I looked at my mother's kind face, I wondered whether she might have become independent out of necessity. I knew she had been lonely. "I had good friends at church," she explained, "but I was so ashamed of where we lived that I didn't want people to visit us. My sisters never had problems bringing their friends home, but I did. I always had the feeling I wasn't quite measuring up."

"Doesn't sound like you were getting your needs met," I suggested.

My mother looked thoughtful as she explored this idea. "My dad was drinking until I was eleven—and I know Mother was ashamed of the way she was living because she had grown up in a secure family that adored her. She was the 'diva' and thought of herself as 'number one.'"

"Really?" I was beginning to see my grandmother in a slightly different light.

"According to my aunt, my grandfather told all his children, 'You are number one,'" explained my mother. "My mother was adored because of her voice and her piano playing. She was a very social person with a lovely style of relating to others. But she didn't make me feel like I was adored. I didn't grow up with a sense that I was number one—and that could have been because of alcoholism. I think Mother had been used to being put on a pedestal before she got married, but she didn't get that in her marriage. Daddy adored her, but he also had four daughters. Mother seemed needy."

Then she told a story I was surprised I hadn't heard.

"When I was in junior high school, Mother went to one of my afternoon choir concerts," she began. "This particular concert was a big deal because there were a lot of kids and I was proud of being part of it. As we walked out of the auditorium, my teacher told my mom that I was an exceptional musician. I could read music well and was more of a leader than the others."

"What did your mother say to that?"

"'I have three others at home,' was her only comment," answered my mother. "I remember just turning away because that hurt; it took the wind out of my sails. When I look back on it, I think Mother wanted to be the center of attention."

I remember my grandmother as a firm but loving adult—an extrovert who made doll clothes for her granddaughters, taught piano, and loved to show off her strong, high soprano. Sometimes when we drove to Minnesota from Tulsa or St. Louis, we would visit her in her apartment near downtown Minneapolis. Other years, she would come to our house and sit with me at the piano as I learned to play. My mom seemed happy to see her, but as I grew older I also thought I detected anger and annoyance when my mother talked about Beth.

I had mentioned the subject to my mother many times over the years, and she was always pretty matter-of-fact about it, so I asked again more directly. "You've always seemed kind of mad at your mom," I offered. "Is that why?"

"I don't know if 'mad' is the word," she responded. "Maybe it's 'respect.'"

"Say more."

"Mother was sick quite a bit of the time when I was younger," recalled my mother. "I don't remember that she cried a lot normally, but she did when she lost Tommy, who was stillborn."

I knew that wasn't the only child Beth had lost.

"And that was the second death," confirmed my mother. "At that point, Daddy was probably drinking a lot. He was a traveling salesman for a few years, and had bought a house but had to sell it because he couldn't make the house payments."

I knew firsthand what it was like to live with an alcoholic. But I couldn't fathom the sorrow of losing two children.

"I think it was depression that made Mother cry," she continued. "When I was three, she went into the hospital for some kind of test and had to stay there because of a flu epidemic. Nobody was allowed to come in or go out." Then Mom added, "I did find letters when we were going through papers after she died. Daddy wrote a couple to her when she was in the hospital." She smiled as she recited more of the details. "They were like love letters, and he was telling her about what all of us kids were doing." Her smile faded as she added, "But he didn't mention me, and I remember how that hit me hard. Another letter said I was at my Aunt Edie's house at the time, though, so maybe that was why."

I was getting the impression my mother felt left out much of the time she was growing up. And I strongly suspected it had something to do with her father's fondness for alcohol.

THE DAY WE drove to Ste. Genevieve, we had started our conversation over coffee at a quaint, well-known restaurant along the way. The story got more interesting at the winery in town and continued to expand over tea and chocolate cake as we sat together in the lovely B&B garden. That's when she filled in details I hadn't known about my grandparents—like the fact that they had been very much in love right up until my grandpa died a year after I was born. We went on discussing her childhood during cocktail hour, held in the beautifully restored French dining room. That's when I learned more about her older sister, Doris, who had shouldered more responsibility for her father than I had ever realized. And now, here we were having *more* wine at an attractive new dinner spot right down the street. What better time to examine the alcohol problem that runs through several generations of my mother's family?

I knew it was time to talk about Joe Fristedt.

Edith always described her parents as being "loving and wise." That said, she had also admitted that their struggle with Joe's chronic alcoholism left them less able than most to attend to the needs of their children, especially during the Great Depression. As Joe continued to frequent the local bars with some of his brothers—also alcoholics—his family was forced to move into increasingly shabby quarters.

Many times over the years I had asked my mother how she felt about her father's drinking, and she had always replied she didn't remember being affected much by it. But after losing a sister in the 1990s, Mom began talking about it with her other two sisters. And suddenly they were all more willing to answer questions, especially since some of their own children had struggled with alcoholism. So in 2015, when I asked again about my grandfather's drinking, my mother had a different answer.

"The shame I felt about where we lived went deep, but I didn't feel disgust when Daddy was drinking," my mother began. "I do remember hearing him stumble up the stairs from time to time . . . and a lot of the time I guess he just wasn't there mentally."

She paused for a moment before continuing. "He kept a bottle in the storeroom just off the kitchen, and I remember he'd walk in there during the day—I'm sure to take a drink. He was working part of the time, but he didn't have a job he ever went off to."

"How did his drinking affect your sisters?" I asked.

"I know Doris often had to go find him in the bars and bring him home when she was growing up," answered my mother. "And Phyllis remembered seeing him stumbling down the middle of the street one Sunday morning after a long night of drinking."

"So when did he stop?"

"Well, when Doris announced her engagement, she told Daddy that if he had been drinking when he came to the wedding, she would ask her future father-in-law to walk her down the aisle," explained Mom.

"So what happened?"

"He had one navy blue suit that stank," remembered my mother. "But for Doris's wedding he got it cleaned. And he walked her down the aisle sober. Shortly after that, he joined Alcoholics Anonymous. The brothers he drank with eventually joined AA, too."

As we talked about her family, my mother's voice became quieter. "It must have been hard for Mother," she said toward the end of dinner, "especially when she compared our situation to her own childhood on the farm, where she was surrounded by three sisters and six adoring brothers."

Reaching back to childhood recollections of my grandmother's siblings, I could still visualize her brother Jess, a cheerful man we saw occasionally when we lived in California during the late 1950s. He always wore a cowboy hat and string tie. I also remember Auntie Phi. Eleven years after Joe died and a few years after losing her sister, Grandma had married Phi's husband, Ben, and moved into his house in Nashwauk, Minnesota. But the one who made the strongest impression on me was my mother's Uncle Howard, whose enormous family still lives in Grand Rapids, Minnesota. I'll never forget the year I attended a Watson family reunion, where Howard and his wife and family welcomed me to their lakeside celebration with open arms. *After growing up in a family like that, Grandma must have loved Grandpa very much to stay with him,* I thought. I also understood how difficult it would have been to leave her marriage. And I was glad she hadn't.

Unfortunately, Joe's happy ending created a new challenge for my mother when Beth turned her full attention to her husband's sobriety. With one sister married and the other two pursuing active social lives, eleven-year-old Edith was left to fend for herself.

She had a hard time describing what that was like. "I guess I didn't think about it at the time. I probably needed my parents, but they were gone a lot after Daddy got sober," she said. "So I got really involved at church."

That's right, I thought. My mother still talks about how much she had loved being with her second "family" at Simpson Methodist Church—a spiritual environment that provided her with a level of confidence and direction she would depend on for the rest of her life.

Then I thought about her faith. My mother has never tried to force her Christian beliefs on anyone, including her children. I didn't notice that as I was growing up, of course. I knew my parents expected us to go to church, but my mother never attached her ego to her children's spiritual lives—she herself always loved going to church, always sang in the choir, and found her closest friends within that community. When she married my father, she became a Lutheran, but she continued to demonstrate her faith through a quiet tolerance and generosity I've always attributed to her Methodist upbringing.

And for some reason it's only as I face my own aging process that I realize how my mother's example has affected me. I see her strength and the light that shines through her eyes; I feel the love that comes from her heart; and I know—because she's told me so—that the power and brilliance behind her clear, beautiful voice come directly from her God.

Maybe it's my God, too. Not just because I've noticed that the two women among my subjects who lived the longest were lifelong members of a faith community. Or in spite of well-meaning relatives who have tried to talk me into accepting their views. I have my own thoughts about God these days, and my own experiences. Even my grandmother—the person whose views I rebelled against most—encouraged me not to be concerned about what others thought. And Hallie, who told me never to compromise my own values. I may not belong to a church, but I do know God in the way I know God. My mother accepts that, which makes me love her even more.

MUSIC IS A language my mother has loved and understood from a very young age. "I had been told I was good at music but never believed it," remembered Edith, who began taking piano lessons at age six. "Mother once told me that my teacher, Mrs. Royal, had me playing songs not long after I started reading music—and that she had me play the music backwards because I read it so quickly. It's hard to understand, but I remember doing that and even remember the book. I would look at the music and play from the end of the song to the beginning." Years later, my mother found out that when Beth spoke to Mrs. Royal about her daughter being "difficult," her teacher replied kindly but firmly, "Let me take care of it."

Edith knew her mother was widely admired for her music and sensed that Beth didn't wish to be upstaged by her youngest daughter. "Did she compete with all of you?" I wondered.

"Not with Doris," said my mom. "Doris's personality was more like Mother's."

I thought about how my grandmother's relationship might have been different with her oldest daughter—the child who had most likely experienced happier times with her parents; the outgoing, fun-loving beauty queen who sometimes had to search for her drunken father when he didn't return home. How much did Beth depend on Doris? And how much guilt might she have felt about what her daughter had been required to do?

Those are all things my mother wouldn't have seen or recognized as the youngest child. For Edith, one unspoken rule seemed clear: She was not to upstage her mother or any of her sisters when it came to music.

My mother's resilience and independence served her well when she turned to the large and welcoming community at Simpson Methodist Church. She spent many happy hours practicing with the choir and performing with her sisters. As a teenager, she also took piano lessons from the choir master, who told my mother she should be singing soprano.

"I couldn't believe it when I found out I had a voice and could be a soloist, because I never thought about or wanted it. And I didn't think I could hit any high notes," said Mom, who usually served as alto lead in every choir she had joined. Ironically, it was the highest notes that would thrill Edith's audiences for the next sixty-five years—notes she hit clearly, powerfully, and without the tremolo that distinguished her mother's style. As a musician, my mother had become her own woman.

In spite of her talent, however, my mother says she backed away from challenges she thought she couldn't meet. "I took voice lessons from Mrs. Zimmermann, and she suggested I audition for Rupert Circum," remembered my mother. "He was the well-known and highly respected choir director and organist at Westminster Presbyterian Church."

"You mean that enormous church at the corner of Hennepin and Oak Grove?" I asked, thinking about the high-profile social and political events that were still held there.

"Yes," my mother confirmed. "Rupert wanted me for soloist, but he wasn't the only one on the committee. So when a woman who was more of a performer got the role, he asked me to sing in the choir as an alto part leader. When he found out I was also a pianist, he asked me to accompany the choir for one rehearsal when he was going out of town. But I was scared to death and said no because I didn't have the confidence."

As I listened to my mother, recollections of my own aversion to performing washed over me. I remembered one night as a seven-year-old when I feigned sickness to avoid doing a cartwheel in front of the PTA meeting my parents attended. In seventh grade, I dropped orchestra class to avoid the short, in-class solo I knew I'd have to perform when it was time for me or another student to move up to the next "chair" within the violin section. And when I refused to go for the high note in "Summertime," the song from *Porgy and Bess* that we were asked to sing during a high school choir audition, I missed out on two years of singing with the senior choir. I was even too proud to accept the offer extended a few weeks later by one of the choir's two directors to sing with the group anyway.

Suddenly I felt compassion for my mother, and a slow thawing of an icy internal voice—the critic that admonished me silently every time I replayed one of those painful scenarios in my mind.

Mom continued: "I was given opportunities that I never

accepted or wanted, so I never stuck with any one church for long. I was soloist in the Unitarian Church for a month, then in the Episcopalian."

"Why did you do that?" I asked.

"I think it was too much commitment for me; for example, when I sang for the Episcopalian church, I got laryngitis on the day I was supposed to hit a high C. I knew I wouldn't be able to do it, so I just quit. I didn't stick with things." Watching her face, I knew there was more.

"I'm not sure whether I gave notice or simply said I can't do it anymore. Those are things I don't remember . . . maybe on purpose," explained my mother, shaking her head.

"What about the time you wanted to sing for the University of Minnesota?" I asked. I had heard pieces of this story before but had never understood exactly what happened.

"Well, I went to audition for the University choir and they gave me music to read. When I made one mistake and stopped to apologize for it, they didn't know what to say. The music was difficult, so of course I made a mistake . . . but I couldn't accept that and they must have seen my lack of confidence."

"You were hard on yourself and expected perfection," I said, relating to the feeling far more than I wanted to admit.

"I did get into the evening choir and sang with them," said my mother, finishing the story.

That brought to mind the time I auditioned for the well-known choir at the small college I attended after freshman year. The famous director had determined I had talent but not enough experience—I'd need to sing with the chorus for a year and audition again the following year. He even encouraged me to do it. As before, however, I was too proud. I told myself it would be too much work with no guarantees. And for some reason, I didn't want to mention it to my mom that night, either—I was angry at both of us. I had given up the chance to stretch myself musically and now

I understood that my mother had done the same. But she had only walked away from a few opportunities; she continued to sing. I had stopped singing altogether.

THAT EVENING I told my mother I was getting the idea that while her sisters and parents enjoyed singing with her, they weren't very involved in her life otherwise.

"They weren't," she agreed. "And there were no other girls around I could play with. The only girl I remember was ten or twelve years old and she came from a completely different type of family."

"What do you remember about her?" I asked.

"She smoked. And one day she gave me a cigarette on the front porch of our house right there on Nicollet Avenue. Mother came down and saw me, but never said anything because she knew I wasn't interested."

When I showed surprise at this, my mom explained. "You know, Mother was not real controlling as a parent. I knew she was there, but I don't remember having discussions with her." I thought of my grandmother as being both verbal and in charge, so that didn't fit with my image. Then my mother said, "She tried to help me with singing and piano lessons and I wouldn't listen to her. She finally gave up trying to help me. I didn't want help."

I was beginning to see another side of my mother, one that was confirmed when she looked at me and said matter-of-factly, "I was rebellious."

"Rebellious" is not a word anyone I knew would use to describe my mother. Her friends would say she's "fun," "talented," and "friendly," but often fairly quiet. The ones who know her well might see her stubborn side, and I would add "silly" and "creative" to the list. But I doubt whether more than a few people have actually seen my mother rebel.

"Inside I was rebellious," she began, "but I learned to be cautious about showing that side of myself because I knew I had to be responsible for what I did, especially when it came to lying. I knew lying would come back to me."

Itsy had learned about lying the day she ran a tube of salve around the dining room walls inside her family's apartment. "Daddy asked whether I had done it and I said no," explained my mother. Although Joe didn't reprimand her, he somehow persuaded his daughter to admit to the deed. A few days later, he also got her to admit to adorning the walls a second time. "My parents were never harsh, but I felt shame because I knew I was wrong," recalled Mom. "To this day I can't lie about anything."

Months after the interview, I talked about the incident with a child social worker and walked away understanding that my mother's behaviors could have represented legitimate anger at being neglected and dismissed.

But that day when I asked for other examples of childhood rebellion, my mother brought up the accident on Twenty-Eighth Street, a story I had heard about throughout my own childhood.

"Following Stanly Perkins down that alleyway when I was only five or six . . . would a child with any common sense run across a busy street?" my mother wondered, shaking her head. "I would call that impulsive," she added, forgetting that many children of that age might do the same. "I knew I shouldn't cross. Normally I was careful because I had to cross that busy street when I went to school."

That's when I remembered a lingering question I had about the accident. "Where were your parents when it happened?"

My mother paused and looked down as though she were watching a movie of that long-ago day. "They were in the car together driving home on Twenty-Eighth Street when I got hit," she began. "Later I found out they were in the line of cars that had to stop because of the accident." After another pause, she added, "Mother was nine months pregnant . . . and she lost the baby, a little boy, a few days later. His name was Tommy."

When she raised her head, I saw my mother's face grow sad. Trying to put the pieces together, I had a horrible thought. "Mom, you didn't feel responsible for your mother losing that baby, did you?"

"Maybe I did," she answered softly, eyes widening at the thought.

My mom had always said she had trouble expressing anger. And she still can't cry for herself. She was loving and attentive as a mother but had trouble comforting us physically after we reached a certain age—certainly by the time we were teenagers. And it all made sense if my mother had believed at age six that her own anger was powerful enough to kill her unborn baby brother. She might have felt like she needed to squash those feelings whenever she felt herself getting angry.

Once she grew up, however, Lord help the child or adult toward whom my mother's righteous indignation was directed—those may have been the only times she allowed her stuffed anger to emerge. My father, who often but not always deserved it, had already served as her main target for close to sixty-five years by the time she and I talked about it.

I suspected that my mother's suppressed rage had something to do with her difficulties around speaking up in a group setting. She often described being at a loss for words; my guess is that she was still stuffing feelings.

~

My parents love to tell the story of their whirlwind meeting and courtship; the topic comes up at every family reunion and even during most conversations with visiting relatives. But no one has ever asked for details. I knew my mother had continued to live at home after graduating from high school and that she was working as an elevator operator when she met my father. But I didn't know where or how it happened.

"I was working at the Rand Tower in downtown Minneapolis,"

she began. "I didn't know your dad or his friend, Frank—the one who thought Dad might be interested in me."

"How did Frank know about you in the first place?"

"I worked with his wife, Jean, who was also an elevator operator," explained my mother. "They got engaged and when she asked me to sing at their wedding, I agreed to do it. That's how I met Frank."

I had never understood this part of the story, so getting it straight was important. "How did Dad know him?"

"They both worked for the railroad and Frank told your dad he thought we would have a lot in common. I guess Dave used to ride in my elevator and watch me, although I wasn't aware of it," recalled my mother.

That's when I decided to ask my father for details.

Mom had been correct: He had been working for the railroad downtown when his friend, Frank, encouraged him to ride Edith's elevator. My dad had noticed the girl with "the beautiful blue eyes," but considered Edith to be out of reach. However, he liked the idea enough that he began waiting in the lobby until he could ride her elevator to the fifteenth floor.

About a week after my dad had started watching her, Frank mentioned that Edith was going to Chicago over the coming weekend to visit her sister, and would also be seeing her boyfriend. When my mom wasn't wearing an engagement ring the following Monday morning, February 26, Dad spent the week rehearsing what he would say and finally worked up the courage by Friday to call her. They went to a movie the next night, March 3rd.

After that, things heated up fast. Their second date was Sunday, March 4th, and while they had to skip Monday, they saw each other for the next three nights. On Thursday, March 8th—their fifth date—my parents were engaged to be married. They had known each other for less than a week.

Somehow, I had remembered a three-week courtship—five days was a little more alarming, although by the time I had the details straight my parents had been married for sixty-four years.

"So you had no idea who Dad was when he called you?"

"No, I didn't," Mom answered, giggling. "In fact, I'd never heard of him and only had an idea of who he *might* be when he told me over the phone that he got off the elevator on the fifteenth floor."

"Wow, that really *was* a blind date," I said, asking myself whether I would ever have done the same. *Probably not,* I surmised.

"So how did you feel when you finally met him?" I asked.

"Well, I recognized him as one of two guys who got off on the fifteenth floor. And I was relieved to see who it was!"

"And how did you know after that short a time that you wanted to marry Dad?" I asked my mother.

She thought for a moment before speaking. "Neither one of us has ever been able to give a specific answer to that question," she said. "Two or three other guys had asked me to marry them, but I had turned them down. With your dad, I just knew he was the right one. We wanted to be together all the time from the very beginning, so we didn't even talk about it."

And that was all I needed to know, because finally I had the story straight:

First date on March 3rd; engagement on March 8th; engagement ring on March 16th; church wedding on June 23rd, 1951.

On June 25th, 2016, David and Edith Egertson celebrated their sixty-fifth wedding anniversary at a beautiful restaurant on "The Hill," a famous Italian neighborhood located in downtown St. Louis. In attendance were their four children; two daughters-in-law; one unofficial son-in-law; six grandchildren with their spouses, fiancés, or significant others; and a small group of close friends.

I REMEMBER A childhood filled with sunshine as we moved from one warm climate to another. My father's career at the Frisco

Railroad was progressing rapidly, and each time he got transferred, my mother looked forward to a different life in a new state. Some women, myself included, would have disliked the packing, cleaning, unpacking, and arranging required to move every few years. For my mother, that was the adventure. There were always questions: What would the new house be like? Where would her children attend school? What new people would she meet? Where would she buy groceries, and where would her new church be?

But during each transition to a new city, my resourceful father would carefully research all of those questions and have the answers by the time his wife and family arrived to inhabit the house he had chosen. This process was repeated every time we relocated: from Minneapolis to St. Louis, Missouri; then to Fullerton, California; on to Tulsa, Oklahoma; and finally back to St. Louis, where my parents lived until well after all four children had graduated from high school.

I knew what my own answers would be to each of the questions I had prepared for my mother about raising her family, but I wanted *her* perspective.

"How would you describe your style as a mother?" I asked. It took her a few moments to find the answer. "I wanted to be sure you kids knew right from wrong," was her first response. That sounded right to me. I have vivid memories of having my mouth washed out with soap when I said "shut up" to one of my younger siblings. Twenty-five years later, students in the seventh-grade English class I taught would lose points or be asked to leave the room if I heard them use that expression.

My mother also used spanking as a disciplinary measure, in spite of the fact that her own parents neither raised their voices nor struck their children as punishment. "Why did you spank us?" I asked at one point. "You didn't grow up with that."

"I don't know why I did that," she said after a long pause. Maybe spanking was related to her need to teach her children right from wrong—and she did that vigilantly. Later, I thought of another reason: it could have been another way to express repressed rage. Her spankings weren't matter-of-fact. She was usually truly angry, which hurt more than the swats themselves.

"But I loved you from the moment I knew I was carrying you—it was a natural instinct," she added. "As a mother, I wanted to nurture and it came naturally."

I agreed that nurturing her children physically came naturally for my mother—we were well-fed, warm, neatly dressed, and attended to meticulously when we were sick. But my mom didn't know how to attend to our emotional needs or help us succeed in school—she hadn't received those things from her own parents either.

I remember the day one of my aunts told me she had always thought that my siblings and I must have experienced a perfect childhood with Edith as our mother. I thought that was an odd thing to say until I realized that from the outside, we must have looked like a perfect—and perfectly healthy—family. And for the most part, I believe we were.

"I took my job as mother and homemaker very seriously," Mom continued. "I felt it was a positive role and always knew what I wanted to do without even thinking about it."

That's where she is truly confident, I thought. But what I asked was, "How did you learn to be a mother?"

"I'm sure I learned from my own mother," she answered. "Mother was wonderful and very loving. I trusted her and knew she would always be there for me when I needed her."

"Perhaps physically, but certainly not emotionally," I mused.

"I was a very confident parent," Mom added, "even though I can remember only one time I had to take care of a baby as I was growing up. I knew nothing about it and didn't think about children. But when I got married, I knew I wanted to do it."

I had heard stories like that from other women and felt like that about my own daughter. I enjoyed babysitting as a teenager but had little real interest in children until I had one of my own.

"I had said I wanted four children," she went on, "which might have shocked Dad, but he didn't argue. And I didn't think about having any of you until I was pregnant."

"What do you mean by that?" I asked, not sure I understood. First of all, I couldn't imagine "knowing" I wanted to give birth four times—although I realized that was an average number of children during the fifties, everyone knew having babies was physically painful. And caring for four of them would be exhausting. I also wasn't sure I thought it was such a great idea to simply have babies without planning for them, even a little. What if my dad had lost his job? What if one of the children—or one of my parents—had gotten sick? I hadn't really thought of my mother as a "confident" person, although she certainly seemed to be in charge when we were little.

"I didn't think about things ahead of time—I reacted instead of planning," explained my mom. "So we didn't talk about when to have children before I got pregnant each time. I guess I didn't know how to plan or set goals," she admitted.

That made me feel better—she hadn't been flip about not planning her pregnancies. "I believe that's common among children growing up with alcoholism," I said. "Besides, I'm sure there weren't a lot of birth control options in the 1950s."

"I did use birth control," said my mother. "But there were four nights—only four—when we talked about having children briefly. Those were the nights I didn't use birth control. And those were the nights I got pregnant."

Attempting to wrap my mind around what that meant about my mother's fertility, I repeated what I thought I heard. "So you're saying you got pregnant every time you didn't use birth control?"

"Yes," she said, still sounding a little amazed after all these years. "We'd talk about having a baby and I'd go without birth control one time and that night I'd get pregnant." Then she added, "Of course we were both thrilled about it each time."

As we laughed together, I remembered something else I'd heard her talk about many times. "You've said those were the happiest years of your life. What was so good about them?"

"When you kids were growing up, the mothers in our neighborhoods spent more time at home with our children—not like now, with all the extracurricular activities that require parental involvement," she began. "So I also had time to decorate and handle the house as I saw fit. And your dad and I had no conflicts around raising you kids—we always decided things together."

That was true; my parents were always in sync when it came to us.

"You kids were wonderful," she said emphatically. "You were all healthy and just fun to have around. And you did obey me—I was very strict."

There it was again. "More strict than your own parents," I offered.

"Yes," she agreed. "And I'm not sure why." Neither one of us seemed willing to explore that area further, so we returned to the discussion of what she loved.

"What happy moments come to mind as you think about raising your children?"

"Christmases were always fun," she said, adding an explanation I hadn't heard before. "I would plan them, decide on gifts, make dresses, buy things for Dad . . . and I wasn't judged."

Feeling "judged" had become a theme throughout our interviews, although that didn't surprise me. I knew she was talking about my father at the moment; I also knew my mother's unconscious rules against showing anger seemed to prevent her from challenging her husband when she disagreed with him. Without a way to express her opinions, she would understandably feel judged. And she was right about the holidays, which were busy but somehow less stressful than other times.

"Christmas in our house was different from the way it was when I grew up; when you kids were little, I was in charge. I made the decisions and was able to be creative," said my mom.

I recalled those years with great fondness. During the week before Christmas, we would spend hours making sweets—that was one time during the year when we didn't have to worry about how much things cost. At some point, Mom would drive us up to the local strip mall, where we would use our allowance to shop at Ben Franklin and the Creve Coeur Pharmacy for gifts. Later we'd have fun taking turns wrapping gifts behind closed doors; there were plenty of supplies, too. My mom may not have planned ahead when it came to having babies, but she was always ready when it was time to wrap presents.

I assumed most families had "programs" too—we had to dress up in costumes for ours, which also included singing Christmas carols around the piano and listening to the Christmas story. I'm sure my siblings and I fought as we were getting ready for church, and we still groan about the program. But that was our own special ritual, one we could count on doing every single year. My dad was happy because it reminded him of his own childhood; my mom was happy because we were singing; and that meant the rest of us were happy, too. As with all children, opening presents was the ultimate goal, but as I grew up and moved away from home I came to think that the best thing about Christmas was a deep sense of unity and wellbeing we felt as a family. Despite the cold, dark weather, the six of us were truly happy together. We didn't need anyone or anything else on that night, and it was my mother who made sure it all happened. No wonder she loved Christmas. As the author of our festivities, she had created one of the happiest times of the year for her family.

BIRTHDAYS, EASTER, AND Thanksgiving were equally festive—and when we entertained our grandparents or overnight guests, my mother was clearly in her element.

"I loved those times because I liked being in charge and enjoyed spending time with the people who came to our house," said Mom. "It's strange to even say that because I've never thought about it. We had lots of people stay with us, and you kids were always a part of it. I loved seeing everyone being happy, being fed, and having fun."

I was surprised too, listening to my mother—and given her skill and experience, which I watched throughout my childhood, I wasn't sure where my own performance anxiety around entertaining had come from. I was also surprised by Mom's answer to my next question: "What was hardest about those years?"

"When your dad was out of town, I felt free," she began. "But as soon as he came home, I felt nervous because he wanted to know about what I was doing."

I believed my mother felt judged, but something about her description confused me. "Asking about your week sounds like a normal question," I said. "And you've said you and Dad didn't have conflicts about raising kids—so what made you feel judged?"

"I would start to stiffen up just knowing I wouldn't have control over decisions—what we did and didn't do as a family or socially . . . things like that," she explained. Just as I was about to challenge whether she thought my father truly wanted or expected to make all the decisions, my mother added, "The minute he got home, I turned over my authority to him."

That felt terribly—and painfully—familiar. I knew that in spite of how well I could write and speak up in school, I had often clammed up too, within both of my marriages. No wonder I had felt so conflicted about getting married—on the one hand, choosing a partner for life and raising a family together felt like the right thing to do. On the other hand, I believed I would automatically lose power—if my mother hadn't known how to express herself at critical moments, how would I know how to use my voice and exercise my power within a relationship?

"But I'm also proud that most things at home went smoothly," my mother said. "Your dad and I supported each other and worked together. We were so proud of all our children—not because of what you did but because of how balanced you were."

"Does that mean you think we were well-adjusted?" I asked. Once again, I saw what others probably admired: a good-looking, healthy family that seemed to have fun together. And while that was true—we were still having fun in our sixties—each of us had dealt with anxiety that manifested in adulthood as alcoholism, overeating, digestive disorders, or workaholism.

"Yes. You were good kids—all four of you liked other children and were good to others," continued my mom. "I have always been proud of how loving and caring you were as children, and of who you became as adults."

Our childhood hadn't been perfect, and each of us had dealt with addictions or physical challenges tied to our emotions. But as my mom presented a new and powerful view, my perceptions of my childhood slowly began to shift and heal. I had dealt long ago with the pain and doubt that I carried into adulthood, and hearing my own mother describe me as the type of person I myself aspired to be was powerful. Very powerful indeed.

"Is there anything you wish you would have done differently?" I wanted to know.

Clearly prepared for this question, she answered at once. "I wish I had been more demonstrative with you kids—especially with your older brother."

When I asked her for an example, she said, "I have the feeling I quit touching and hugging the boys after a certain age, and especially your older brother. By the time your younger brother arrived seven years later, I understood boys better. I just wish I had known earlier about how to show my love."

How would you know how to show love when you hadn't experienced it yourself? I wondered when I read through the interview later. But that day I merely nodded my head in agreement, remembering how hard my parents had sometimes been on their oldest child. I also knew those feelings and relationships had been addressed and repaired over the years.

As our time for the interview came to a close, I had a final, more sensitive question for my mother—something I should have asked years earlier. "If you could offer advice about raising children, what would it be, Mom?"

There were plenty of times in the past when I wouldn't have wanted to know the answer to that question—times when I struggled as a parent.

"I'd say do what you feel is best and try not to worry about what other people think about what you did or how you should raise your children. If you believe you're doing what you think is right, stick with it."

When I thanked my mother for saying that, she simply nodded her head, acknowledging in silence the problems I had faced as I tried to be a good parent while navigating an alcoholic marriage. My mother had understood far more than I had given her credit for. And I realized I was witnessing, in that very moment, what stands out about my mom—a woman who has always been able to see and recognize the best in any of her children. A woman who models daily the deep tolerance and acceptance I continually strive to exhibit within my own life.

~

Most women I meet who are my age and younger—and certainly those I am closest to—either dreaded or will dread the onset of middle age. Personally, I will never forget the day I saw a close-up of myself in a video I was putting together for an internal audience at work. I was so shocked by the dark circles under my eyes and the skin beginning to loosen at my chin line that I pulled myself out of the video completely. I was forty-six at the time.

Today I'm shocked when I hear about women in their thirties who feel the need to correct whatever flaws they see on their faces as they get older. As women, we seem to hate how we look as we age.

I thought my mother would feel the same way, but when I asked her whether reaching middle age was difficult, she looked a little surprised—and told me "middle age" itself was never a concern. It's what happened *during* middle age that bothered her.

My older brother and I were away at college when Mom turned forty-five, so I wouldn't have known what she was experiencing at home. As my younger teenage siblings pursued an active avoidance of school and increased social activity, my mother continued to care for the house, make clothing for herself and others, attend choir and Bible study at church, and plan and prepare all meals. She cooked a full breakfast every weekday and packed bagged lunches for each of her children throughout our high school years. That didn't leave her with a lot of time, so when her poker straight hair needed a wave, she'd give herself a home permanent; when she needed a haircut, she'd make an appointment at whichever beauty salon was closest. Beyond that, my mother paid little attention to her appearance.

Apparently, my father was paying attention.

David Egertson is an observant man who has always known what he wanted and considers every option when making a decision. When he has an opinion, he offers it directly; this is what he was raised to do. And he brought those behaviors to his marriage.

Adept at both written and spoken communication, David did well in business. But that style didn't work as well at home, especially with a wife who struggled to believe her opinion mattered. To this woman, her husband's views mattered above all others. So a sharply worded comment designed to add clarity when directed toward a spirited group of high-level executives would have felt overbearing to my mother. Especially if it contained an opinion about her appearance.

My mother was about to describe one such time.

"Dad has always professed his love, and I believe him," said my mother, recalling a specific incident that had deeply affected her. "He has always told me I am beautiful, so I didn't worry about getting older or losing him."

"He's always been a pretty handsome guy," I added, thinking about how dapper he still looks in a suit.

"Years ago, I could tell when he was attracted to another woman," continued Mom, "but I never took that seriously because he always let me know how he felt about me."

She also didn't know my father expected his wife's role to extend beyond homemaking as he moved up at the railroad. "There was one time in particular that changed things," said my mother. "Your dad was expected to attend an important company dinner and spouses were invited. I had made a blah-looking skirt for the event and I wore no makeup."

I remembered some of the items my mother made for herself; most were simple, some close to nondescript. "What happened?" I asked, with a sense of dread.

"He was upset with me," she answered. "Didn't I think enough of him to dress up more, is what he asked," she recalled.

Instantly, I felt conflicted: On the one hand, I didn't believe my mother should base her appearance on what would make my father look good; on the other, I could relate to why he would have wanted her to care. I also remembered how my mother downplayed her natural beauty. In spite of the good taste she showed in choosing clothing for her children, the clothes she made or bought for herself seemed at times to be severely plain.

"I was all ready to go out and I didn't realize I looked like a frump," said my mother. "I must have, though . . . I'm sure the colors were not flattering and I didn't wear makeup. I don't even remember the evening," she added. "I was more than willing to go to the dinner but didn't think about showing your dad my outfit ahead of time. Besides, I was always worried about buying and paying for clothes, so I made simple things for myself."

I'd been in that place myself at times. But unlike my mother, I knew I looked frumpy the minute I tried on an outfit. In high school and college I had known exactly what looked good on me. Once I was married, however, I lost my sense of style. I also had a recurring nightmare about clothing—a dream that felt like it lasted for hours. It always started with me standing in front of a closet full of clothes – dozens of items I could choose from to create a fabulous outfit. Then I would try on everything—literally every item in the closet, and in every possible combination. But nothing looked good; I always looked terrible after hours of trying to put an outfit together. And I would wake up feeling both discouraged and exhausted.

The day I interviewed my mother, however, I was remembering the beautiful clothes she had created for me and my sister; I'll never forget the gorgeous velvet dress she made for my tenth-grade homecoming dance.

As we talked, a series of images came to mind—a photo I had seen of my mother as a young woman, dressed in a perfectly fitted suit she had made for herself; another photo of her as a teenager, sitting on the lawn in shorts and a crop top. One of my favorites shows her standing with her sisters in a soft, feminine summer dress. I compared those images to the film clip my family always giggles at together, of my mother wearing a rubber swimming cap with floppy flowers on top and a strap fastened tightly under her chin. She wore that to our swim club with a conservatively cut plaid swimming suit that camouflaged her still-shapely body. *What had happened*? I wondered. *Why had she changed?*

I became even more uncomfortable when I thought about how I had altered my own appearance during my first brief marriage. One day, after cutting my long, healthy locks in favor of short, unattractive layers, I was shocked by my reflection in the mirror.

When I realized I had also swapped my flattering, perfectly fitting jeans and T-shirts for baggy trousers and unattractive tops in colors and fabrics I didn't like, I felt depressed. And I didn't know why I was doing it.

Then I remembered something my mother had mentioned casually during a previous conversation, when she told me she had never thought of herself as being beautiful. I translated that to mean no one had told my mother she was attractive as she was growing up. Later, physical appearance simply wouldn't be a priority for a woman like my mom, whose number-one job as a mother was to care for her home and children. Unfortunately, I turned that into an unconscious rule about how I should "dress down" once I got married. And I held onto that belief until a therapist helped me realize I didn't need it anymore. I never stopped feeling annoyed about what a great haircut and wardrobe cost, but decided I would always be willing to pay for them.

Returning to the conversation with my mother, I asked, "So what happened after that night?"

"My confidence had been shaken, so I started using Merle Norman cosmetics," she explained. "A dear friend from church helped me choose the makeup; she also reminded me of my best features."

Thank God for Betty, I thought, remembering how lovely Mom's friend from church always looked.

"I bought new outfits, too," she continued. "Your dad helped me pick out some of them. And I found a good stylist who cut my hair for many years after that."

I thought fondly of the fun, hip man who had subsequently styled my hair as well as my sister's. I also recalled a photo from that time period, of my mother dressed in something black and elegant, her dark hair softly framing a face illuminated by makeup and glasses chosen to enhance her incredible eyes. Had she reinvented herself for my father? Or did she use her anger to give herself permission to take care of her appearance? Perhaps both. In any case, she seemed to like the results.

These days my mother pursues her own style more often and has a better sense of what looks good on her. Sometimes she needs help choosing jewelry, but for that she has me, as jewelry has become my obsession—one I am more than happy to share with my beautiful mother.

~

Once my younger siblings had moved out of the house, my mother spread her wings.

"You were in a community play performed at my high school," I said, remembering my mother in her stage debut as a cheerleader dressed in a short skirt and pink sweatshirt—the one I eventually confiscated and wore until it fell apart years later.

"Yes, that was fun," she said.

"How did you get into that?" I asked, finding it hard to believe that my mother would try out for a play on her own. "And did you want to do it again after that first time?"

"I think a neighbor told me about it," she recalled. "So I auditioned and got a role. We all sang and then I was one of three or four cheerleaders. It was fun, but I only wanted to do it once."

"You went to community college too, didn't you?" I asked. I knew she had kept a cardboard collage depicting her life, which she had assembled for one of her classes.

"I did, because I wanted to get into music therapy," she explained. "But I had to produce my grades from high school and couldn't remember where those were; so instead I took one year of classes—in music appreciation, choir, music theory, and English 101. I did well in all of them."

I remembered how energized she had seemed about that.

"So why did you stop taking classes?

"I loved college, but I thought your dad was uncomfortable with me working in your brother's old bedroom by myself, so I quit after one year. I also remember telling Dr. Lauber about music therapy, and he said hospitals weren't using it. That threw me."

I thought back to our house in St. Louis and tried to imagine what it would have been like for my parents to live there without kids. Mom would have had every weekday to herself, to attend classes and do her homework. I'm sure she would have devoted some evenings to homework as well; but did my father really care about where she did it? I could imagine he might have been annoyed with any adjustments to his schedule, especially if that meant his wife was less available during evenings and weekends. But I believed he would have compromised. I also knew if his tone had been at all condescending when he expressed his opinion about her activities, my mother would have had neither the language nor the courage to defend her point of view. Not even when it had to do with what she herself wanted.

And an opinion delivered by the kind, soft-spoken physician who had attended to our family for well over a decade would have been important to my mother as well. I know he would have stated his point of view matter-of-factly. I also believe he would have felt terrible if he had known his comment had so powerfully discouraged my mother from following her dreams.

And that's exactly what drove me crazy: Why did it matter so much to my mother what my father thought about how she was spending her time while he was at work? And why would she give up something she wanted to do because of what one person—someone who had absolutely nothing to do with music therapy—had said? Why did a man's voice always carry more weight with my mother than her own?

Maybe she needed to find her voice, too. What the hell had happened to the women in my family?

I was lost in memories when my mother said, "I didn't think it was working at home for me to be in school . . . I didn't discuss this with your dad, but I didn't go back."

She didn't discuss it . . . because she didn't know how to express her needs and it never occurred to her that she could ask someone else to compromise about what it might take to meet them. I hated that tendency in myself, especially since I constantly found myself doing what I thought someone else wanted when they hadn't even asked for it. If they knew what it cost me—what I was giving up to please them—they would be mortified.

At times during my life I had blamed my father for holding my mother back. Five months after the trip to Ste. Genevieve, however, I was starting to notice a pattern in my mother's behavior that felt uncomfortably familiar.

I knew that when my mom wanted something badly she could usually figure out how to set things in motion. People responded well to her warm and open personality, so she has always been quite popular in any group. But when something she wants becomes difficult, as things do with almost anything important, my mom tends to back away from it. She has often said she doesn't like conflict and has complained all her life about a lack of confidence—and I've always hated hearing about that.

At the time of the interview, however, I believed communication may have been the bigger problem. I recalled something my mom had told me about her relationship with her own mother and I scrambled to find my notes.

"I didn't want to be like Mother and speak as slowly as she did," my mother told me early on in our interview process. "She went into such great detail about everything she talked about. Even when she was telling details of her day, like the people she had seen or talked to, she would look around like she had to think about it. She spoke distinctly and was articulate, but I wanted her to talk faster."

"What didn't you like about that?"

"I think I was impatient," she explained. "It took Mother so long to express her thoughts that it was sometimes hard to listen to her—and my sisters felt the same way." Before I could connect that comment to the struggles I knew my mother had with sharing her own opinions, she added, "I've tried not to be that way, but I know I am to some extent. My thoughts just don't come to the surface—I have a lot of anxiety about it."

I knew this was true; my mother had mentioned more than once that this inability to articulate her thoughts was happening to her more often. She said the frequency scared her and made her self-conscious. She was also well aware that over the years her family had wondered whether she was suffering from mild dementia. When I observed her more closely, however, I noticed that she only became unfocused in response to emotional stress. In my opinion it was anxiety—not dementia—that forced her into silence or forgetfulness.

Returning to her childhood, my mother said, "I never felt like I could talk with Daddy, either. But then I didn't talk with anyone or even ask questions because if I didn't get the right response I would just shut down. That's been something in me since I was little."

When I asked for an example, she said, "Once when I was in high school I asked Daddy a question about math and he said, 'Well, have you really studied it?' After that I didn't want to go any further. I think he had helped my oldest sister too much and decided he shouldn't help the rest of us at all. But I didn't want to be rejected, so I didn't take it further." Just as I was thinking that my grandfather would certainly have helped his daughter if she had answered his question, my mother added, "Being rejected was a pretty big theme, so I stayed aloof. I loved people, but I didn't pursue any friendships."

That made sense, too. My mother is a beloved member of many groups, but no one can remember her having a best friend. Perhaps she didn't know how to do that. I knew she had felt close to her sisters, and especially to Phyllis. But were they really close? Or did my aunts see their little sister more as a pet?

"But you're so social," I countered. "You love to be with people and they love being with you."

"I think I've learned over the years that it works both ways; I've realized that I'm worth it to some people—that I AM important to some people, and that can really feel good."

Struck by the magnitude of that statement, I tried to mask my alarm. *She must not see or value her other talents,* I thought. Then one talent in particular came to mind—one that neither of us spoke about much in front of others, although we had often discussed it when we were alone. My mother calls it ESP—extra-sensory perception, for anyone too young to recognize the term. I'd call it a natural energetic openness . . . an ability to serve as a channel between the Divine and those she loves.

In its simplest form, my mother knows when things are happening—like the day she felt a sharp pain in her head at the exact moment my older brother injured his head in a car crash. Or the Sunday night in 1974 when I sat crying beneath the phone in the hallway of the house I lived in during college, wishing my mother would call from St. Louis because I couldn't afford the long-distance charge. When the phone rang abruptly, I got to my feet and picked up the receiver, expecting to hear a request for one of my roommates. But as I wiped my tears and said, "Hello," I heard my mother's urgent voice on the other end. "What's wrong, Jenney?" she asked, without even bothering to find out which of the eight girls living in the house had answered the phone. She simply knew.

I'm sure my mother attributed these gifts to God, somehow—maybe I rejected that idea because it seemed like she was turning over her power to yet another male authority figure. The ultimate male authority figure. The language Lutheran congregations repeated every single Sunday seemed to be infused with male energy and described a God that judged His subjects as being worthy or not. At one point I refused to repeat some of those lines; and I looked for spiritual groups or practices outside the church that would incorporate my natural talents.

I also believed I had inherited some of those talents from my mother—like the things she can do with her hands. Houseplants that receive my mother's attention bloom prolifically; I believe they also benefit from the energy conducted through her warm hands. And her prayers. When a person or animal she loves is sick, my mother says she directs her thoughts of healing through God to ease their pain.

I have always understood that kind of healing as a transference of energy, and more aligned with Eastern medicine. In the 1970s I had a fascinating conversation with a physicist, who told me he thought the universe was more than a vacuum or void. He believed space had substance and that energy, which included thought, could travel through it, from one spot to another. Whether or not that's really what he meant, it's all I needed to hear; I was sure my childhood belief in magic had just been converted to science. I told myself that if thought could affect physical objects, then what we called magic was actually the result of a change in energy. I knew that was quite a leap, but it made sense to me and I didn't really care what anyone else thought. The notion that thoughts affect matter also formed the basis for my interest in Eastern medicine and energy healing. Eventually, I came to believe that my mother was using the same principles when she prayed, or demonstrated ESP. I perceived her to be a natural healer.

I felt the effects of her healing ability myself one time, when I asked her to participate in a group effort to focus energetically on a digestive problem I was having. I had arranged to have eight people, including my mother, direct their thoughts, prayers, energy—whatever they believed in—toward me and a specific part of my body at a designated time. They would do this together from wherever they were across the country for twenty minutes. During that time, I lay on my bed and meditated, opening myself to receive the energetic healing. As I calmed my mind, I felt a great sense of peace and saw a gentle pulsing of lavender light—a common visual for me when I close my eyes in meditation. And then I heard something I hadn't expected. A voice. In my mind I distinctly heard someone talking. And I knew who it was because I recognized my mother's clear, confident words. She was instructing the other participants directing the healing.

"Did you know you were taking charge?" I asked later, when I called to get her feedback. Most of the other participants had employed various energetic techniques used by practitioners of Eastern medicine—techniques my mother hadn't studied. But that didn't seem to bother her. "No, but you're my daughter," she replied. "I guess it makes sense that I would lead."

My mother was important to others, all right, but I wanted to make sure I understood what she had meant when she said she hadn't always known that. "So, for much of your life, you believed that your opinion didn't matter?"

She nodded. "When did that start to change?" I asked.

"I think it's been within the last twenty to thirty years."

That would have begun in her mid-fifties, long after I was out of the house. I knew my mother had made attempts to improve her confidence and verbal skills, at one point even wanting to sign up for a Dale Carnegie course. That was something we had in common.

"I took a Dale Carnegie course to get over stage fright," I said when my mother told me she had considered doing the same thing. I also knew my father thought a lot of Dale Carnegie. "It made a huge difference to my career."

Unfortunately, Mom never took the course. "Dad said he was afraid I'd never finish—that I'd give up—so I backed down once again," she explained.

Something deep inside you must have been afraid he was right, I thought. "Maybe he was trying to be realistic," I offered.

Apparently, all it took to talk my mother out of pursuing something she wanted was a challenge or expression of disapproval on the part of an authority figure or someone who mattered to her.

And my father would have been both. I knew from my own experience that he was capable of stopping a conversation cold with a disapproving comment or tone of voice. I also knew he responded better than most to feedback when that happened, and that he often seemed genuinely surprised by how his words and tone affected others. My mother wouldn't have known how to offer feedback. Still, I wondered, *Why did she give up so much control?*

"I believe now that when we got married your dad was looking for a mother and I was looking for a father," admitted my mom. "He has always had strong opinions about me and what I do. I'm able to recognize and deal with that now, but back then I gave up easily and didn't know how to ask for help."

"You seemed pretty independent as a child," I said when we talked about this. "When did you start to defer?"

"Growing up, I never let anyone take advantage of me or push me around. Your dad is the only one I have ever let control me, and that's because I love him," she answered.

That explanation seemed suspect, so I asked for more details. I had no doubt my mother loved my father; I also knew that people often give up control to avoid being abandoned. My mother had just confirmed that she had found a father in my dad, and he a mother in her. Neither could stand the thought of being abandoned again, so there would have been every reason in the world for them to stay together.

"I knew from the first time it happened during our engagement. I shouldn't have capitulated when your dad told me he didn't want me to stay for the reception after a wedding in which I was singing," she explained.

"So you wanted to stay," I said. "I can understand that. But do you know why he wanted you to leave? Was it because, as you said earlier, the two of you just wanted to be together all the time?"

"Maybe so," she said. "I probably would have been able to discuss it with him, but I didn't give him the chance. I just agreed immediately. He was the first one who mattered that much . . . so much that I didn't even think of what I wanted except to please him."

You could never risk being left by Dad, I thought. Pleasing him was my mother's choice, and in that context it made sense. But her choice to remain quiet affected their relationship. If she didn't know what she wanted, how could my father have known what his young wife was feeling?

As she continued to talk, I saw the innocence in both my parents' actions—behaviors I had witnessed and incorrectly interpreted for my entire life. Because by the time I noticed them, my mother was *angry.*

"I never wanted anyone to take charge," she continued, "so I was probably cutting off my emotions when your dad would tell me what he wanted me to do. I was betraying myself by not expressing what I wanted, but I don't remember having awareness of that at the time." After a long pause she added, "Maybe I thought I would be left or abandoned."

There it was. "Well, you've said more than once that rejection is a big theme in your life," I observed. "And back then you probably didn't have the language you needed to articulate what you wanted. What was the dynamic between your mom and dad—did one of them give up easily?"

"I think my dad did," she said. "Mother never did. I remember hearing that he didn't do well selling insurance because he couldn't ask his friends to buy from him. But when he joined AA, he did very well. He was asked to speak often and did it beautifully." Then she added, "You would have enjoyed talking to your grandpa, but I never could. I think he believed he had done too much talking with my older sisters, so he didn't talk much to me—but I could have used more help."

I was so sad for my mother when she said that; she had felt ignored by the most important adult in her life other than her mother, who talked too much anyway, in Mom's opinion. All my life I had watched my mother struggle for words. Often, when she wanted to contribute to a conversation, I would see a series of emotions play quickly across her face: first consternation, as she tried to find the words; then frustration, as she wasn't able to do it fast enough; discouragement showed up next, when she gave up trying; and finally her face registered anger if my father or someone else answered the question for her.

I, on the other hand, had learned from both my parents: like my father, I could read, write, and speak quite eloquently. Sometime in my mid-thirties, however, I began to have panic attacks in settings where I was expected to comment—at work, in class, or even in more casual settings if the group were large enough and I cared about what the other speakers thought of me.

Suddenly my mother's behaviors—and also mine—made all the sense in the world. Mom hadn't gotten what she needed from her father, whom she believed didn't want to hear from her. I doubted whether that was true, but could imagine how it happened. To compensate, she married an extremely articulate man who could speak for her—she would both depend on that and rail against it. She would defer and then be mad about it. I carried on that particular part of the legacy by marrying a charming, handsome alcoholic who was so adept with language that I lost most of our verbal battles. I'd always put up a good fight; but like my mother, I typically lost in a war of words with my husband, whom I still refer to as the "walking dictionary." And that would help explain my discomfort with marriage in general—unconsciously, I believed the husband always had the upper hand. That wasn't true for my brothers—their wives could both more than hold their own verbally. But in my world the rules were different for boys and girls; after two tries at marriage I would never take that chance again.

~

IT WAS 1981 and I was in my late twenties when my parents moved back to Minnesota. My father's company had merged with another railroad, and he and my mother decided to relocate while he looked for a new position. After seventeen years—the longest time they had ever spent in one city together—they packed up their belongings once again. However, this time it was my mother who worked full time, while my dad looked for a job.

"I remember driving up to Minneapolis to visit you at your townhouse," I said as we reconstructed those years. "You worked for an insurance company, didn't you?"

"Yes. I was in the typing pool," she replied. "Before I applied for the job, I borrowed an electric typewriter and got my speed up to ninety-one words per minute with one mistake." Mom was one of about eight people in the typing pool and among the first to start working on a computer.

"Some of the lawyers wanted me to type their letters," she added. "But there was some jealousy among the other typists about my getting ahead like that, so I quit."

"You quit over jealous coworkers?" I asked, amazed.

"Yes," she answered matter-of-factly. "One lawyer even asked me to be his secretary, but I was ready to stop. I think I worked there for a couple of years."

In a later conversation with my father, I learned that once he had secured a senior-level position with the Soo Line Railroad—which happened shortly after they arrived in Minneapolis—he and my mother began building a house. Apparently my mother was ready to go back to homemaking, the job she loved most.

But I had a few more questions: "How did it feel to be the breadwinner? And how did that change the dynamics of your relationship with Dad?"

Her answer surprised me. "It was okay; Dad said I should spend that money on myself, but I never could," she explained. "I didn't think of myself as the breadwinner, and when he got a job, we pooled our resources. It's not part of my nature to spend money on myself. I still have trouble with that."

And I had a strong reaction to *that.* Apparently, my mother felt fine about depending on my father financially. Entitled even, which made sense according to their lifelong agreement about roles within their marriage.

Unlike my mother, however, I had never—underline *never*—wanted to be without my own source of income. I would *never* allow another person, especially a husband, to support me. I was *not* good at housekeeping, was *not* good at meal planning or preparation, and did *not* see myself as being what I would call a "natural" mother. I was so afraid of losing power that I burned through two marriages—one to a man who might have supported me had I wanted that, and the second to someone who had neither the means nor the desire to be the sole breadwinner.

As the facts of my mother's life settled in, I had to admit that even had I wanted to be a full-time homemaker and parent, I could not have allowed myself to pay what I believed would be the ultimate price: a complete loss of power, control, and self-esteem.

That thought brought to mind the aunts, cousins, and sisters-in-law who had chosen full-time parenting and homemaking versus a career outside the home. I certainly didn't think less of them, and I've always admired the lives they built for themselves. But that's not a view I applied to myself, as I examined what having money meant to me. The answer emerged as a painful set of questions:

With no income of my own—money I had earned—how could I expect to have a say in any decision-making? I didn't believe I could.

What would give me the right to pursue my dream of being a writer, if it meant sacrificing income? I was sure I had no right.

How could I respect myself were I to become seriously ill or disabled and someone else had to pay my medical bills? (The thought still terrifies me.) I would rather die.

How would I support myself when my husband divorced me as I became old and unattractive? I believed that was inevitable.

And then the real question emerged: *Without my own income, what would be my worth as a human being?*

The startling answer: *I would have no value.*

Apparently, I had assumed my father's values about money and my mother's battle for self-worth. And it would continue to be a deadly and discouraging combination until finally, in my sixties, I would gain enough confidence to exercise my voice and finish what I started. I had given up my voice at age four—that awareness came as a result of working with Maude. My grandmother's disapproval forced me to fight for my vision and my approach to the work. I felt loved by Sadie, and gained strength from her resilience and her commitment to her community. I still feel deeply connected to Ruthie, who helped me to be a better parent. Hallie gave me courage and the determination I needed to "press on" with my dream. And my mother—my mother gave me life in the first place, and will remain my champion until both of us are gone.

In 1986, my husband and I decided to move to the Twin Cities with our two-year-old daughter to provide her with access to good public schools and at least one set of grandparents. When my father called to tell us he had retired from the railroad and would be looking for another job that might take him away from Minneapolis, we said we'd come anyway.

We moved from St. Louis in June of 1986 and lived in my parents' basement for the next three months, taxing their patience and hospitality. Finally, and with no time to spare, we found, bought, and moved into a house conveniently located next door to my cousin. A few weeks later, my parents left for Cleveland, where my father had accepted a position he would keep until he retired (again). Sad as I was to watch my mother leave, our relationship had been stretched to a limit we had never experienced and weren't used to navigating. Life with three unemployed adults and a toddler had been hard on Edith, whose anxiety was triggered by her son-in-law. With less than three years of sobriety under his belt, he had replaced his compulsion to drink with cigarettes, coffee, and the bear claw pastries he bought every morning on his way home from driving me to work. My mother reacted to his addiction and I reacted to her.

I had taken a low-level job with an insurance company while my husband cared for our daughter—a role reversal that was hard for my parents to accept. Once again, my mother watched a woman she loved support a man who was not providing for his family the way she believed he should. Within a few months my husband found a full-time job, which enabled me to work at home as a consultant; but by that time my parents had moved.

Recently, during a conversation to verify the dates of their moves, my father described the time he and my mother spent in Cleveland. "You remember the house we had in Shaker Heights, don't you?" he asked.

"I do," I answered, recalling the sunny black-and-white kitchen, the warmth of the upstairs bedrooms, and my parents' stories about Matilda, the ghost who knocked their clock off the wall and opened their music box occasionally. It was my favorite of all the houses they've owned.

In addition to caring for the house, my mother quickly found her place within a well-established church, located in downtown Cleveland. She became a member of the choir immediately and attended the weekly Bible study for women. "She was actively involved with our local Welcome Wagon, too," said my dad. My mother used to talk about the packets she made for new arrivals to Shaker Heights, and how much she enjoyed welcoming new families to their community. While my father handled marketing and operations for a mid-sized technical company, my mother enjoyed a full, independent life. She seemed especially happy and vibrant during those years.

When my father retired for good five and a half years later, he and my mother had to make a choice between moving back to Minneapolis and returning to St. Louis. They knew I had moved my family to Minneapolis to be with them. But while they were gone, I had found a neighborhood "family" on Eleventh Avenue South, living among like-minded teachers, social workers, and artists. I was also close to my grandparents and the aunts, uncles, and cousins on both sides of my family who lived in Minnesota. So I felt a mixture of disappointment and relief when they chose St. Louis, where they could live near two of my siblings and three grandchildren. They knew my sister, in particular, would need their help as her son grew up in a single-parent home.

Within weeks, my mother settled back into the community she had left eleven years earlier. Her beautiful home had plenty of space for gardens; situated between her children, it was also close to her beloved church community, which had continued to grow and thrive. For the next dozen years, my parents' lives were filled with purpose as they provided support for my sister and watched my brother's family blossom. They made time for adventure, too, traveling to Florida, Scandinavia, and continental Europe in between annual trips to Minnesota and California to visit their other children and grandchildren.

Finally, when my parents tired of yard work in their late seventies, they moved into the perfect townhouse, where they adopted a cat, remained active in the church, and worked as hospice volunteers. In their early eighties, they took their entire family to Florida for their sixtieth anniversary. Eventually life slowed down for my mother as she began to address the inevitable effects of aging.

These days she takes an afternoon nap with her faithful cat Sassa Nea sleeping at her side. Although she retired, at age eighty-five, as lead soprano for the choir, she still sings with the church octet. She also sings with a group that provides musical comfort for hospice patients who request this soothing blend of voices at the very end of their lives. She still attends both church and Bible study once a week and book club every month. In addition, she joins my father as they minister more and more often to their sick and dying friends. So many from my childhood are gone now.

And I—I still have *her*. At age sixty-four, I know how lucky I am to have grown up with a mother, to *still have* a mother, and most of all, to have *this* mother. I also know that while I am not my mother, I am the woman I have become *because* of my mother.

So I thank this beautiful woman—Edith Norma Fristedt Egertson—from the bottom of my heart. The heart that began in her body. The heart that will always belong next to hers.

ACKNOWLEDGMENTS

To MY WONDERFUL family: my parents, Dave and Edith Egertson, who told me every step of the way that I could do it; my original partner in crime, Kyle Radcliffe, and our daughter, Rowan; my loving partner, Kevin Volk; my siblings, Jeff, Vonnie, and Joe, who kept me honest; my aunt and uncle, Bonnie and Joel Egertson, who had the guts to tell me the truth for eighteen years; and the many other relatives who reviewed chapters and offered encouragement.

To the dear friends and mentors who supported me throughout this journey: Mark Looker, Ann Aronson, Jack El-Hai, Ann Bauer, Kelly Chatman, Mary Regan, and Jody Hilgers, among many others

To the people who trusted me to treat their mothers, aunts, grandmothers, and mentors with dignity and respect: Beth Kelly, Tony Mefleh, Joyce Yamamoto, Carol Johnson, and Bernadeia Johnson.

To the talented professionals who helped me to organize, edit, produce, and market my manuscript: my editors, Peggy Henrikson and Erik Hane, and my publishing mentor Dara Beevas and her talented team at Wise Ink.

And most of all, to the amazing women who told me their stories and gave me permission to age: Maude Kelly, Irene Egertson, Sadie Anton, Ruth Yamamoto, Hallie Hendrieth-Smith, and Edith Egertson.

This book has come to life because of you.